Surf City

The California Sound

The Life, Times, & Music™ Series

SURFERS
DON'T MISS THE
DICK

Surf City
The California Sound

The Life, Times, & Music™ Series

Jack Wood

FRIEDMAN/FAIRFAX
PUBLISHERS

Acknowledgments

The author would like to thank the following people for their assistance, patience, and time: Bob Keane of Del-Fi Records, for the interview; See Hear (New York City); the staff of the Brooklyn Public Library; "green pen" Ben, for the extensions; and Ted and Anna Springett, for their attic. Special thanks go out to Rob Santos, for all the info, pictures, and leads, and extra-special thanks to Liz, for putting up with the hours and hours of surf music.

Dedication

To Brian Wilson

A FRIEDMAN/FAIRFAX BOOK

ISBN 1-56799-186-6

Editor: Benjamin Boyington
Art Director: Jeff Batzli
Designer: Tanya Ross-Hughes
Photography Editor: Emilya Naymark
Production Manager: Jeanne E. Kaufman

Cover photography credits: The Beach Boys: © Michael Ochs Archive; Annette Funicello: © Photofest; Jan & Dean: © Frank Driggs Collection/Archive Photos; Teenagers with convertible: Courtesy of Oldsmobile; Wave: © Bob Barbour/Tony Stone Images

Grateful acknowledgment is given to authors, publishers, and photographers for permission to reprint material. Every effort has been made to determine copyright owners of photographs and illustrations. In the case of any omissions, the publishers will be pleased to make suitable acknowledgments in future editions.

Printed in the United States of America by Quebecor Printing Semline, Inc.

For bulk purchases and special sales, please contact:
Friedman/Fairfax Publishers
Attention: Sales Department
15 West 26th Street
New York, New York 10010
(212) 685-6610 FAX (212) 685-1307

CONTENTS

INTRODUCTION

"You heard the last of surfin' music."

—Jimi Hendrix, June 18, 1967, the Monterey Pop Festival

During his appearance at the Monterey Pop Festival, guitar legend Jimi Hendrix predicted the end of surf music; this was not only a reflection on the music industry, but a direct reference to the absence of the Beach Boys, who had canceled their appearance the previous night. They were unable to be there, they said, because they were busy in the studio and guitarist Carl Wilson had a meeting with the draft board the next week. The truth, however, was that Brian Wilson, the leader of the group, felt that the band was out of sync with the times and would be ridiculed.

Surf music achieved its greatest popularity from 1961 to 1965. By 1967 the political and social climate in America (and the world) had changed dramatically from what it was in the early sixties. There was a war going on, drugs were in vogue, and, within the space of only a few years, surf music had peaked in popularity.

For the United States, the decade had started with a new president and the promise of a New Frontier. There was still the threat of nuclear war, but the militaristic atmosphere in the White House was somewhat diminished by the departure of Eisenhower. His successor, the charismatic John F. Kennedy, was the youngest man ever elected to the presidency, and he had an even younger wife and two small children. The Soviets remained the villains of choice, and the United States was involved in a race with them into space.

California was still young in relation to the East Coast. The mass exodus to the West in the 1920s and 1930s had resulted in parcels of land covered with tract homes, faceless

For many emigrants to California in the middle of the twentieth century, tract homes were a relatively inexpensive option for a new home.

By the late 1950s, the television was a common feature of most American homes.

housing projects with no center. The majority of youth in southern California were either first- or second-generation residents. California was the Promised Land, a place to start over. Parents had taken their children there so that the kids would not grow up worrying, as the parents had, about food, clothes, or creditors knocking on the door.

This was the setting for the rise of surf music. The biggest worry most of these teens had was whether they had a date for the next school dance. Some kids worked after school, but not because they had to; most of these kids took jobs because they wanted to save money to buy a car, or perhaps a guitar.

Television was becoming commonplace in homes across the country, and with television came rock and roll. While radio had also been a great vehicle for promoting these performers, television gave the kids faces and bodies to go with the voices of their favorite singers or bands; teens could actually see the rock and rollers they admired (without having to go to a concert), and what they saw was that the stars were not much older than—or much different from—themselves. Soon, kids were volunteering to clean out garages with the understanding that room was being made for a drum set, not for the family car.

With a few exceptions, the surf music scene was confined to the southern coast of California. Very few surf bands ever toured outside Orange County, and those that did found mostly puzzled audiences at the venues. The Beach Boys and, to a lesser extent, Jan & Dean, became the rest of the country's idea of what surf music was all about. The defining characteristic of surf music is probably the use of the guitar—whether as in the aggressive attack of Dick Dale's "Miserlou" or the melancholy loneliness of the Chantays' "Pipeline"—rather than vocals, as the melodic lead. A general description of surf music would include phrases like "guitar-driven instrumentals," "reverb-soaked recordings," and "indigenous West Coast music, 1961–1965." Surf musicians, however, would give a more abstract view; the music was (and is) meant to evoke the mood of surfing as well as the act itself. Surf music was the soundtrack to that sport and to a particular era in American history.

As is the case with any localized, short-lived movement or trend (whether musical or social), surf music is very hard to research because of the obscurity of even the major players and the lack of historical documentation. Many bands were around for only six months before they splintered, sometimes re-forming into new bands, sometimes abandoning the music world altogether. The relatively inexpensive recording scene had many groups releasing singles on labels that folded after only one or two releases. And because most of the band members were still in their mid-teens when they were most popular, not many thought to document the period.

DICK DALE (1938–): KING OF THE SURF GUITAR

Dick Dale, pictured here in 1963, paved the way for countless surf bands.

Surf music began as an instrumental subgenre of rock and roll. While there certainly were instrumental bands before surf bands came along—the Rumblers and the Ventures, for example—it was Dick Dale who made the first attempt to re-create the feeling of surfing with the electric guitar. Many groups claim to have recorded surf songs prior to this time, but Dick Dale received the press and was dubbed "King of the Surf Guitar." Seemingly overnight, kids were getting Fender guitars and reverb units and starting their own surf bands.

Born Richard Monsour in Beirut, Lebanon, Dick Dale moved to Quincy, Massachusetts, with his family when he was a child. His father, Jim, started the young Richard on piano when the boy was nine. Later, Richard taught himself to play harmonica, trumpet, and guitar. His guitar idol at the time was Hank Williams, whose songs about loneliness and solitude had great appeal for the young man.

When Dick was a senior in high school, his father moved the family again, this time to El Segundo, California, a suburb of Los Angeles. After high school, Dick went to work at Hughes Aircraft and joined the National Guard. Urged by his father, Dick entered some of the contests at the local country bars; he won one and joined the house band as the trumpeter (there was already an overload of guitarists). Eventually tiring of his lack of guitar time, he quit the gig and entered another contest, which he also won. The name Dick Dale was suggested to him by a four-hundred-pound L.A. DJ known as T. Texas Tiny. Dick thought this name was better suited to a country singer than his given name, so Richard Monsour became Dick Dale.

In the meantime, Jim Monsour had started a label, Del-tone Records. In 1959 Dick released a pair of vocal singles on this label—"Ooh-Wee Marie" b/w "Breaking

A multifaceted performer, Dale not only played guitar but also sang and played piano, harmonica, and trumpet.

Heart" and "Stop Teasing" b/w "Without Your Love"—and in 1960 he released a few more. (These releases have resurfaced, much to his dismay, at various times in the past thirty years.) His recording of an original, "Jessie Pearl" b/w "St. Louis Blues," marked the turning point in his career—this release was his last before he became involved in the surf scene. Up to this point, Dale had seen himself as a vocalist rather than as a guitarist. His popularity after he turned to instrumental music gave him a new focus both in the recording studio and onstage.

Balboa Peninsula, located down the coast from El Segundo, was the typical California hangout in the early 1960s. In late 1960 or early 1961 Dick and his cousin Ray Samra started playing afternoon shows—for free—at the Rinky Dink Ice Cream Parlor. These shows became quite popular, and the owner of the Rinky Dink soon hired Dick and his growing band, which he had named the Del-tones, for eight dollars a night plus free Cokes and 7-Ups.

Dick Dale & His Del-tones, circa 1961-1962 (left to right): Bill Barber, Rick Rillera, Nick O'Malley, Jerry Stevens, Dale, Armon Frank, Barry Rillera.

Hanging Out In The Early Sixties

Prior to the 1950s, most teenagers' spare time away from school, church, or family meals was usually spent under the watchful eye of an adult. Few parents would let their teenagers go to their friends' houses if there were no parents at home. The one–working parent household was still prevalent and mothers were everywhere.

With the increasing impact of cars on society, the thought of owning one at the age of eighteen was not out of the question. And even if you didn't own one, it usually wasn't a problem—parents were allowing their teenagers more and more access to the family car for dates and school events.

The 1950s generation of teenagers that grew up in southern California was the first group to epitomize what many adults perceived teenagers to be; movies like *Rebel Without A Cause* and *The Wild Ones* portrayed young adults as selfish, disrespectful, and lazy, and adults were quick to believe these negative stereotypes. The truth was that these were the children of the uprooted and the neighborhoods themselves were little more than a decade old. California was a far cry from "back East," where generation after generation had lived and died in the same block. Here, there was little or no family history or routine. The teenagers of 1950s California were each other's family.

California's weather was as big a factor as any in the free time of teens. It was warm most of the year and kids therefore spent the majority of their free time outside. The beach was the hangout spot of choice. Beach parking lots were crowded after school with hundreds of boys and girls listening to the car radio, trying to get dates, and generally just being kids. Cars, singers, teachers, and the future were all common topics of discussion.

Most of these teenagers fell somewhere between Wally Cleaver and James Dean. There were some who got into trouble more than others and some who stayed home in their rooms, waiting to become adults. But the Vietnam war and the attendant upheaval of the mid- to late sixties put an end to the naive, innocent afternoons of the early sixties. With people dying in Southeast Asia and the civil rights movement in full swing at home, it seemed rather pedestrian to spend one's time simply cruising around in the family car.

Dick Dale, holding a surfboard and surrounded by adoring fans, poses for the obligatory promotional photo.

In 1961 Dick moved to Costa Mesa so that he could be closer to Balboa. He opened a record shop across the street from the dormant Rendezvous Ballroom. His daily routine consisted of surfing in the morning, opening the store for a few hours in the afternoon, surfing again in the late afternoon, and playing a show in the evening. As the crowds got bigger at the ice cream parlor, the band began searching for another venue to perform at.

After Dick was fired by the owner of the Rinky Dink for asking for a raise, he approached Thelma Neufeld, the owner of the Rendezvous Ballroom, which had originally been a big-band dance hall. Neufeld liked the idea of having Dick and his band perform at the Rendezvous, but she didn't think she could pay the group what they wanted. They agreed to split the door charge, which is common now but was unheard of at the time. The first night—July 1, 1961—found a barefoot band playing for a total of seventeen surfers. After one of the surfers asked Dick to start playing some instrumental music, the crowds began to grow. Average attendance rose from 183 in July 1961 to crowds of three to four thousand nightly in August of that year. But Dick's success was not limited to the stage of the Rendezvous; it was around this time that he met guitar maker Leo Fender—who was just starting his empire and whose name would soon become synonymous with the electric guitar—and the two began their mutually beneficial relationship.

The Beast

For over thirty years, Dick Dale has used the same guitar and amplifier. His collaboration with Leo Fender in the early 1960s resulted in the Fender Showman amp and Dale's left-handed Fender Stratocaster, nicknamed the "Beast."

Dick Dale and his indestructible Beast.

Dale met Fender while he was playing regularly at the Rendezvous Ballroom. When the guitarist told Fender that he was having trouble getting the sound he wanted from his guitar and amp, Fender suggested that they begin on-site testing of amplifiers and guitars. According to Dale, they went through almost fifty amps and countless speakers before they found a combination that wouldn't blow up. This model was named the Dick Dale Showman, later shortened to the Showman, and is still a very popular model.

Dale's distinctiveness as a guitarist was not limited to his style or desired sound—he was also left-handed (other noteworthy lefty guitarists include Jimi Hendrix and Paul McCartney). Because of this, he had to flip his guitar over in order to play it. Of course, this meant that his guitar was upside-down, which led to various problems: the volume and control knobs and the pickup switch got in the way of his picking hand, and the input jack for the cord leading to the amp was directly under his left arm, which limited maneuverability; this also meant that the tuning pegs on the guitar's head were on the bottom and the strings were in reverse order (that is, the six strings were set up with the low E at the bottom instead of at the top, which altered the chord patterns and picking techniques).

To get around these problems, Dale asked Fender to make him a left-handed guitar; Fender said it would cost too much to retool the production line, but a short while later he handed the young axman his new instrument: the "Beast." This guitar was like a mirror image of the old one: the knobs, switch, and jack were near the bottom of the body, where they were supposed to be, and the tuning pegs were on the top of the head, as on modern left-handed guitars. Fender also had shaved a quarter-inch off the back of the neck, making it easier to play. Dale retained only one of the unusual features of his old, upside-down guitar: the inverted order of the strings. This was probably because he had gotten used to this order and had already established picking and chording patterns based on it.

Since the day Fender gave him this new ax, Dale claims to have dropped the "Beast" from a plane, shot it with a BB gun, and backed over it in a car. In the early days, he repainted it almost daily; its latest paint job was metallic gold with gold flecks. Recently, an almost exact replica—distinguishable by the surfboard inlay on the neck—known as the "Beauty," has joined the Dick Dale guitar arsenal.

Dale's work with Fender also resulted in his receiving the first Fender Rhodes piano, the first wireless guitar unit, and the first outboard reverb unit, a necessity for that true surf guitar sound.

Perhaps the song most closely associated with Dick Dale is "Let's Go Trippin'." This tune was an unnamed instrumental until he asked the kids at the Rendezvous what he should name it. Their enthusiasm for the song also resulted in a dance known as the "Surfer's Stomp." The original recording of "Let's Go Trippin'" was made on August 23, 1961, at a small studio in Hollywood. A new version (sans the reverb-soaked Strat sound) was cut in September of the same year. Dick's first instrumental release, this song also received credit as the first legitimate surf tune.

L.A. radio ignored the song at first, even though it was getting airplay in other parts of southern California. By December 1961, the song had reached number sixty on the *Billboard* charts. On the strength of this, Dale and the band organized a show at the Los Angeles Sports Arena in early December 1961. This sold-out show drew fifteen thousand fans, a first for a rock band at that venue. On December 23 they played their last show at the Rendezvous Ballroom.

Two more singles followed: "Jungle Fever" was released in March 1962 and "Miserlou" in May 1962. "Miserlou" was the first record to showcase the staccato picking style that Dale became famous for. The success of the singles made it apparent that the time was right for the release of an album. *Surfer's Choice,* a collection

Dick Dale, flanked by his father, Jim Monsour (left), and Capitol Records representative Francis M. Scott, outside Capitol's headquarters shortly after the reissue of Surfer's Choice.

of recordings Dick's father had made of the band's shows, was released in November 1962; it was one of the first albums to feature a surfer on the cover. Also released at this time was the single "Surf Beat." In early 1962 Dale had promoted the album by announcing its upcoming release at concerts; this limited publicity alone generated the sale of eighty thousand records. The sales of the record led to a seven-year deal with Capitol Records, which wasted no time reissuing *Surfer's Choice,* "Miserlou," and "Surf Beat."

The Original Surfaris

The Original Surfaris, circa 1961–1962 (left to right): manager Victor Regina, Chuck Vehle, Al Valdez, Larry Weed, Mike Biondo, Bobby Esco.

The group that became famous as the Original Surfaris started out as the Vogues in Anaheim, California, during the summer of 1960. High school chums Al Valdez (piano) and Mike Biondo (drums) recruited Bobby Esco (guitar) and Doug Wiseman (saxophone), who brought with him Larry Weed, a guitarist who also passed the audition and was asked to join. The group built a local fan base through steady gigging and within a few years had settled into a routine of shows. When local pizza-shop owner Victor Regina saw them play one night, he offered them the opportunity to record a couple of songs at a local studio. He renamed them the Customs and released their first single—"Steppin' Out" b/w "High Hat"—on his own label, Regano Records. Although the two songs were band originals, Regina claimed writer's credit since he had paid for the recording sessions.

Sometime in 1962, the boys saw Dick Dale play and were inspired to try their hand playing surf music. A change of name seemed logical, and it was agreed that the Surfaris was catchy and reflected their new direction. In 1964, however, this name became the subject of a lawsuit when a band from Orange County, using the same name, had a hit with a song called "Wipe Out." In what many perceived as an unfair decision, the presiding judge decided in favor of the band with the hit, even though the band led by Valdez and Biondo had been around longer. He determined that the Orange County band would be called the Surfaris and the Valdez-Biondo group could call themselves the Original Surfaris. In March or April 1963, in an effort to take advantage of the free publicity generated by the lawsuit, Regina rereleased "Steppin' Out" and "High Hat" as "Surfin' 63" and "Boss Beat," respectively.

During the next couple of years, the band continued to record and perform in the Orange County area, even as they went through numerous personnel changes. Also during this time, Tony Hilder, a producer the band had frequently recorded with, shopped the demo containing "Steppin' Out" and "High Hat" to various labels. The group was turned down by many labels who later released the songs without making any payments to the band. Del-Fi released "Bombora" b/w "Surfari," only to have it recalled because it was released under the Surfaris name, not under the court-appointed Original Surfaris tag. The group's name appeared on countless compilation albums with which the group had no involvement. No member of the band received any royalties from the sales of those records or from the sales of those that were legitimate Original Surfaris releases—Hilder had strong-armed the group into selling their publishing rights to him for a dollar a song, telling them that if they didn't sell him the rights their songs would never get played on the radio.

With the band's discography the subject of much confusion and controversy, their cash flow consisting only of door receipts and their lineup in a state of constant flux, the group disbanded in May 1965.

Capitol scheduled a promotional tour of the East Coast for the summer of 1963, but before Dale was sent out on the road the company put out his second album, *King of the Surf Guitar*. As was the custom at the time, the producer of the record didn't want to use the Del-tones as the backing band. Instead, he wanted Dale's musical support to be provided by the Wrecking Crew, a group of seasoned session players who were often called upon to back singers when producers chose not to use the musicians with whom the featured performer had gotten his start. (Hal Blaine, Leon Russell, and Glen Campbell were some of the better-known members of the Crew.) This did not sit well with Dale or the band, but the surf king finally acquiesced and did the album without the Del-tones. The material chosen for the record—another element of this record over which Dale had no control—was of a more pop vocal style, a clear sign that the major labels had no faith in the salability of surf music. Record company executives felt that it might do well in southern California, but the rest of the country was unknown territory.

Because Dale made numerous concessions to Capitol's producers, his first original album for Capitol, King of the Surf Guitar, fell short of his live performances.

The Wrecking Crew

It is common practice in the recording world to use a group of studio musicians, or session players, to record the accompanying music for a vocalist or a vocal group. In some cases, groups of session musicians work together on a number of recordings, thus garnering a name for themselves as a studio ensemble. The Funk Brothers were Motown's house band during that company's early years; Muscle Shoals studios had an unnamed house band to work with artists who needed help achieving their desired rhythm and blues sound; and the Stax/Volt label had a house band that gave their artists a certain sound.

Before the early 1960s, studio musicians had been seen as mercenaries in suits and ties. Their job was to play the music as written, and they were very rarely asked for creative input. Many of the older musicians felt that rock and roll, as a musical genre, was beneath them and played the music accordingly. With the arrival of producers such as Phil Spector, however, there arose a new wave of young session players who were often called upon to give their opinions about arrangements or instrumentation. This new breed of studio player also took a much greater interest in the music being recorded. With the advent of multitrack recording, some songs could be recorded over the course of a few sessions and at different studios. Producers relied on the ideas of the players to build backing tracks, and some

Hal Blaine (foreground, far right) and the Wrecking Crew, in a celebratory mood, hoist producer Phil Spector into the air.

producers were willing to postpone recording dates until certain players were available. Although these players weren't credited on albums, their input and abilities were appreciated by the producers, and as a result they were often given more work than they could handle—some days consisted of four or five recording sessions at four or five different studios.

The Wrecking Crew was the name given to a group of West Coast musicians who were called upon to back hundreds of singers during the 1960s and 1970s. The name was representative of their casual dress and unorthodox approach to recording sessions. The core of the Crew consisted of Hal Blaine on drums and percussion; Ray Pohlman and Carol Kaye on Fender electric bass; Lyle Ritz on upright bass; Glen Campbell, Tommy Tedesco, Barney Kessel, and Howard Roberts on guitar; and Don Randi, Leon Russell, Larry Knechtel, and Michael Melvoin on piano. The Crew also included other players who appeared on some recordings, depending on which instruments were needed for a particular song. The main saxophone player was Steve Douglas, and they had an additional drummer named Earl Palmer.

Since the Wrecking Crew and the surf music industry were both centered in Los Angeles, it wasn't long before some of the Crew were laying down tracks for surf groups. Dick Dale, the Beach Boys, and Jan & Dean were just a few of the artists with whom the Wrecking Crew worked.

Not all the members of the Wrecking Crew limited themselves to working as studio musicians for other artists. Some of them were more interested in building solo careers and weren't always available for Wrecking Crew sessions. Glen Campbell went on to a successful career in country music, Leon Russell made a name for himself as a rock and roller, and some members of the crew, such as Don Randi, have released many jazz albums.

Hal Blaine (right) with session player Glen Campbell, who later had many country hits as well as his own weekly television special.

Because there were no credits given during this time, there is now way to know for sure who played on what track, or indeed how many tracks a given session player appears on. (Hal Blaine claims to have played on 35,000 tracks and 12,000 charting albums.) Since the mid-1970s (and in some cases, even earlier), however, it has become customary for session players to be given credit in the liner notes to the albums they appear on. This is good for two reasons: it gives studio musicians given the credit they deserve, and it enables listeners to learn who is playing backup for their favorite artists and to follow the careers of their favorite session players.

Dale and the band easily filled halls and auditoriums in southern California, but they had less success outside that area.

The tour was disappointing, not only because the album was weak, but also because the music was still relatively unknown outside California. The band played in Boston, Wildwood, New Jersey, and a few other cities on the eastern seaboard, but met with little success. The failure of this tour, combined with Dale's desire to remain home to be near his growing menagerie of wild animals, kept the band from touring. As a result, Dale's music wasn't accepted on a national level.

Despite the tour's lack of success, in 1963 the band appeared in magazines, on television, on vinyl, and in the movie *Muscle Beach Party* (Dale had already been on film before he assembled the Del-tones; he had a small role in the Marilyn Monroe movie *Let's Make Love*). In August, articles about Dale appeared in both *Life* and *Newsweek*. In the fall of 1963, the guitarist appeared on *The Ed Sullivan Show*. Again, Capitol tried to do a makeover of Dale: they had him appear in a suit and without a guitar or a backing band. Sullivan appeared unimpressed with the young innovator: he introduced Dale to the country, let him play his song, then quietly shook his hand and sent him on his way. When they returned to their own turf, the band went back to playing weekends at Harmony Park and Riverside Armory. They also scheduled local television appearances on *The Bob Eubanks Dance Party* and Casey Kasem's *Shebang*. They recorded and released four more singles, including "The Wedge." In November, Capitol released *Checkered Flag*, which was basically a collection of surf tunes with car sound effects in the background.

In March 1964, Dick was the featured performer at America's Third Annual Teen-Age Fair at the Hollywood Palladium. Capitol released the albums *Mr. Eliminator* and *Summer Surf*, spinning a few singles off those LPs. Later that year, Dick and the Del-tones opened the Retail Clerk's Hall in Buena Park. The crowds on opening night were beyond control, and many windows were broken. Eventually, the police had to put a stop to Dale's performances there; he and the Del-tones were replaced by Eddie & The Showmen.

In 1964 the Beatles arrived in the United States, and Capitol put all of their production and promotion energies into that band; consequently, 1965 was not a good year for surf music. All the other groups on the label's roster, including Dick Dale and the Beach Boys, were put on hold, if not altogether dropped. The final Dale recording put out by Capitol, *Rock Out with Dick Dale and His Del-tones, Live at Ciro's* was released in February 1965. Most fans hated the record, feeling it wasn't true to the band's sound. Due to this album's lack of sales, Dick was released from his contract four years early.

In the following months, Dick was diagnosed with rectal cancer. The doctors gave him three months to live, but suggested that major surgery, performed immediately, might save him. This surgery, which consisted of the removal of fourteen inches of rectal tract, six tumors, and seven cysts, was successful. He locked up his shop and his recording masters and moved to Hawaii to recuperate. He credits "the good Lord" with this remarkable recovery.

Steady gigging in the sixties and seventies put Dick Dale in good financial stead. He has invested his earnings in property and has increased his exotic animal count to approximately forty. He now lives near the town of Twentynine Palms, California (due east of Los Angeles, on the border of the Joshua Tree National Monument), with his wife, who is some thirty years younger than Dale, and their infant son. With the resurgence of surf music in recent years, Dale has begun playing the college circuit, which has brought him outside the southern California–Vegas route he had been used to. Because of this, he has expanded his fan base well beyond those who know him and his work from the early days. He has found a new audience among these young people, and he continues to preach the same gospel that he preached in the sixties: live clean and in harmony with everything in nature.

In the 1990s, Dick Dale is more popular than ever: he receives regular play on MTV, is featured on the bestselling soundtrack to the movie Pulp Fiction, *and tours frequently on the college circuit.*

Recently, Dale has tried to distance himself from the new surf music. In the early 1990s, Rhino Records released a compilation of his early work—mostly surf music—which created renewed interest in Dick Dale, as well as a new recording contract. But Dale was not interested in continuing to work in a genre that he no longer felt a part of. He now refers to his music as "Dick Rock" and calls the fans who follow him from show to show "Dick-Heads." Whatever his music is called, his two latest albums, *Tribal Thunder* (1993) and *Unknown Territory* (1994), both on Hightone Records, showcase the fifty-seven-year-old's talents as well as any recording from the early sixties.

THE BEACH BOYS

The original Beach Boys (left to right): Dennis Wilson, Brian Wilson, Mike Love, Alan Jardine, Carl Wilson.

To many music fans, the Beach Boys are surf music. Their many recordings form a certain core of the genre, and their perennial summer tours are a reminder of what summer used to mean. They began their career in the early sixties and they continue to record, tour, and serve as representatives of what many consider the "California Life," even though many of their fans weren't even born when the group saw its greatest chart activity.

The original Beach Boys consisted of three brothers—Brian (1942–), Dennis (1944–1983), and Carl Wilson (1946–)—their cousin Mike Love (1941–), and Alan Jardine (1942–), all of whom lived in Hawthorne, California, a town about twelve miles southeast of Los Angeles.

Brian Wilson showed an interest in music at a very early age. By the time he was three years old, he was able to sing along with songs, almost always singing on pitch. By the time he was in his teens, he was creating intricate harmonies of his own. For his sixteenth birthday, his parents bought him a reel-to-reel tape recorder, and he immediately began overdubbing vocal ideas, using his mother, his father, and his brother Carl as vocalists.

Brian's father and mother, Murry (1917–1973) and Audree (1917–) Wilson, were musicians, and they encouraged Brian's musical efforts and those of their other sons. Murry had had minor success with some of his songs, the pinnacle being a performance of one on the Lawrence Welk radio show. Murry turned the garage into a music room, and eventually Brian moved his bed in, putting it next to the piano.

The year after Brian and Mike Love graduated from Hawthorne High School—at which time Brian was enrolled at El Camino Junior College—they were asked back to their alma mater to sing in a talent show. They immediately recruited Dennis and Carl—to get Carl to perform, they had to name the ensemble Carl and the Passions—and Dennis suggested that they write a song about the surfing craze that was sweeping the beaches of southern California. The song was "Surfin'."

A few months after the show, in the summer of 1961, Brian ran into Al Jardine on the El Camino campus. Brian and Al had both gone to Hawthorne High, where they had played football together and sung in rival vocal groups. Brian told Al about the jam sessions that he was having with Carl and Mike (Dennis, it seemed, would make brief appearances at these jams, but was so excitable that he could never pay attention for any length of time) and invited him to join. Jardine accepted, and the boys got together at the Wilsons' house to harmonize on a few tunes. This initial gathering went well, and everyone agreed that the five of them should start a group. With this, the Pendletones were born.

After the Pendletones had played together long enough to learn a few songs well enough to audition for record company representatives, Al suggested that they make an appointment with Hite and Dorinda Morgan, the owners of Guild Music, a recording and publishing firm in Los Angeles. Al had been to their offices earlier that year to audition with a different group of friends. This earlier group was more in the folk vein, and the Morgans had turned them down. This time Al showed up with the Wilson clan and played a few older tunes, but the Morgans again weren't exactly blown away. Original music was what was needed, they said. Dennis suggested the song they had done at the high school show months earlier, and the Morgans agreed to listen to it. The producers were interested, but told the boys to go home and work on the song, saying that if the revised version was polished enough to be brought into the studio, they would record it.

Apparently, Brian Wilson was a noteworthy character at school. The 1960 Hawthorne High yearbook featured this photograph of him accompanying a couple of his pals on the guitar.

Conveniently, Mr. and Mrs. Wilson were on vacation in Mexico at the time. The band took the money that the Wilsons had left to pay for food and used it to rent instruments. They practiced "Surfin'" all weekend. When the Wilsons came home and found out what the food money had been spent on, Murry went berserk. Eventually, the boys calmed him down and played the tune. Although the song had a rock and roll beat, which Murry did not like, the vocal harmonies were good and it was a fine start overall. Murry saw the band's potential and decided to become their manager. The boys were grateful for his input—at first.

When the Pendletones returned to Guild Music and played their song again for the Morgans, the producers liked the song enough to book time at a studio. The recording of "Surfin'" took all of an hour, and the results were less than wonderful. Because it was the first time in a real studio for the group, everyone was nervous. The group felt that Dennis's drumming was not yet good enough to be used in the recording, and a substitute drummer was brought in; after a few minutes, Dorinda Morgan paid the drummer and had him leave. The recording of the drum track has become a Beach Boy legend: it was performed by Brian; in some stories he plays a plastic garbage can lid for the take, in others he raps it out on a snare drum muffled with a coat.

When it came time to record the flip side of the single, the band found out that the Morgans had already decided what to use: the B side would be an original song penned by the producers' nineteen-year-old son, Bruce. This young man had been writing songs since the age of eleven, and his parents felt that his song "Luau" would make a great flip side to "Surfin'." The Pendletones were hardly in a position to argue, so they did the track.

On the Pendletones' contract with Guild Music, dated September 15, 1961, Brian and Mike signed as the writers of "Surfin'." The royalty rate was low, but the boys were too excited about signing their first contract to put up much of an argu-

The Beach Boys' constant gigging allowed them to bring their highly polished sound to life onstage.

Through their nonstop touring, numerous recording sessions, and constant promotional appearances during the early 1960s, the Beach Boys became the biggest pop band in the country.

ment. Now it was the Morgans' turn—it was time to sell the record. They played "Surfin'" for Joe Saraceno, A&R man for Candix Records, a small label in L.A. He liked it enough to play it for Russ Regen, who worked for Buckeye Record Distributors, the distributors for Candix and many other labels. Regen liked the song but not the name of the group. Saraceno had been calling them the Surfers, but Hi-Fi Records already had a band by that name. Since surf bands were coming out of the woodwork, names were considered in the context of immediate recognition with that trend and record companies felt that the best names were those that incorporated surfing or beach terminology. Regen passed on such monikers as the Lifeguards and the Beach Bums before settling on the Beach Boys. Again the group was not happy, but neither were they in a position to argue—the Pendletones became the Beach Boys and a new legend was born.

The Marketts

The Marketts (the group's name was spelled "Mar-Kets" on the "Surfer's Stomp" single) were essentially a studio creation of producer Joe Saraceno. Using some of the top session players in the Los Angeles area, Saraceno would record tunes under a variety of names, including the T-Bones, the Routers, and the Frogmen. If a particular song was a hit and seemed to deserve a tour, he would assemble a group of young men to learn that song, as well as a few others, and to play a few shows.

The players credited on "Surfer's Stomp" are double bassist Red Callender, drummer Earl Palmer, pianist Ernie Freeman, saxophonist Plas Johnson, and guitarist Rene Hall. All of these players were in and around regular Wrecking Crew sessions; Palmer, in fact, played drums with the Crew, appearing on tunes Hal Blaine wasn't involved in or sometimes accompanying Hal as second drummer.

When "Surfer's Stomp" was produced, the surf craze was just getting started, and the lack of surf tunes on the market at the time helped push the track to number thirty-one in early 1962.

On December 8, 1961, "Surfin'" b/w "Luau" was released on X Records. The Morgans, Saraceno, and all parties involved got to work promoting the release. A few days later, the boys were driving around Hawthorne listening to radio station KFWB on the car radio. The DJ was conducting a popularity contest involving three songs, one of which was "Surfin'." The boys went wild. "Nothing will ever top the expression on Brian's face," said Dennis. "Ever....That is the all-time moment."

Once this song had its radio debut, the Morgans booked the group at the Rendezvous Ballroom for the night of December 29, 1961. Dick Dale & His Deltones were the headliner; other groups on the bill included the Challengers and the Surfaris. The Beach Boys appeared without pay and performed only two songs—during intermission—but even this short gig was good exposure. According to the group and those who remember their performance that night, they were awful, but this didn't stop them from playing a memorial dance dedicated to Ritchie Valens (who died in a plane crash in 1959) two nights later. For this New Year's Eve performance, they received three hundred dollars and some applause.

On March 29, 1962, "Surfin'" peaked at number seventy-five on the *Billboard* chart—not a bad showing for a first-time release on a small label. By the time it peaked, it had sold fifty thousand copies. Murry Wilson was ecstatic, and this feeling was so strong that he gave the Morgans all rights to the band for practically nothing. According to the unsolicited letter-contract that Murry sent to Guild Music, the Morgans were responsible for producing, recording, and promoting the group as they saw fit. But Murry wasn't able to relinquish the reins for long. Even though "Surfin'" was a nationwide hit, he felt the recording was crude and mixed wrong. There was no choice but to become producer for the boys, and what better songs to produce than Murry Wilson originals? If he couldn't be a recording star, then he could get his material heard through the boys—his boys.

In January 1962, the group signed contracts to publish and record more songs with the Morgans. On February 8, they recorded four songs at Keen Studio: "Surfer Girl," "Surfin' Safari," "Judy," and "Karate." At first, Murry insisted that they record a few of his originals, but the band refused and managed to get through the session without recording them. It was also in January 1962 that Brian first met Gary Usher—through Gary's uncle, who lived across the street from the Wilsons. Gary, who was five years older than Brian, had recorded two singles of his own by the time he came in contact with the Wilsons. As far as Brian was concerned, this guy was a seasoned vet, and he and Brian became fast friends. The first evening they hung out together, they composed their first song together. This tune, "The Lonely Sea," would later appear on a Beach Boys album. Over the next few months, the two young men collaborated on over thirty tunes, many of which—"409" and "In My Room," for example—became Beach Boys classics.

Gary Usher was the first of many outsiders with whom Brian wrote songs over the years. He continued to write with Mike Love, but their ideas—both musical

Capitol's promotional department released numerous photographs, like this one taken in 1963, touting Brian's musical genius. In reality, most of Brian's arrangements remained in his head until he got to the studio.

and otherwise—came to differ more and more in the years to follow, and a successful collaboration eventually became impossible. Murry was suspicious of Gary right from the start; he felt that Brian's new friend was simply trying to jump on the Beach Boys bandwagon and that Usher's subject matter was beneath "his boys." Gary and Murry had many run-ins before Murry finally had him banned from the studio. By the time Usher approached the Wilsons on the matter of publishing rights and royalties, he and Brian had already composed "409" and "In My Room," among others. With these successful tunes under their belt, Usher decided that he and Brian should split the publishing revenues fifty-fifty. When Usher mentioned this to his collaborator, Brian said he would discuss it with his father. Nothing more was said about it until Usher brought up the subject again a few weeks later; he was told that Murry had said there was no deal.

Murry must have quickly seen that there might be severe legal ramifications because he soon formed Sea of Tunes Publishing, a company that would manage the publishing rights for songs written by Brian Wilson and Gary Usher, as well as those written by Brian alone or with anyone else. This allowed Murry to create a three-way split—between Brian, Gary, and himself—of the income generated by Wilson-Usher collaborations.

Sea of Tunes Publishing

There is no simple way to detail the responsibilities of a music publishing company. Basically, a music publisher protects, licenses, and administers a composer's catalog of songs. In licensing a song, the publisher decides who can record a particular song and how recordings of that song can be used. If the writer of a song doesn't own the publishing rights, he or she has no control over its use. Michael Jackson, who owns the Beatles' catalog, drew fire from the surviving members of that band (as well as fans of the Fab Four) when he licensed the song "Revolution" to Nike Sportswear for use in an advertising campaign. In a seemingly hypocritical move (considering his reaction to Jackson's sale of "Revolution"), Paul McCartney, who owns several publishing interests and controls the catalogs of several songwriters, licensed Buddy Holly's "That'll Be the Day" to a car company, saying that Holly would probably have done the same thing. In contrast, Neil Young, who owns the rights to all of his songs, has repeatedly refused large financial offers from organizations wishing to use his material for commercial purposes. But licensing is not the primary means by which songs generate income for their publishers. Songs derive income from several sources: sheet music sales, record sales, radio and television airplay (which is tracked by performing-rights organizations such as BMI and ASCAP), and live performances, as well as video sales and the use of music in movies.

Murry Wilson's management of Sea of Tunes Publishing is still being disputed twenty years after his death.

Murry Wilson organized Sea of Tunes Publishing in 1962, primarily to protect the songs his son Brian was writing, but also to provide a means by which he could prevent Gary Usher from receiving his rightful compensation for songs he had written with Brian. Originally, Brian was the sole owner of both the publishing company and the song copyrights. Once the Beach Boys had amassed a few hits, Murry began pressuring Brian into giving up his publishing income. Murry told Brian that he would still make money as a songwriter, but that because Murry was the band's manager as well as Brian's father, he was entitled to the publishing company. After months of being constantly harangued, Brian relinquished 50% of the publishing income to Murry, who also was given responsibility for administering the catalog. This arrangement lasted only a few months, until Murry decided he should be given the other 50%. His first ploy was to tell Brian that he had promised to hand over the remainder to Murry; when that didn't work, Murry withheld Brian's share of the income (the latest check—and this was in late 1964—was for approximately $280,000). Murry told Brian that he was free to take his songs out of the catalog at any time, but he was still obligated to relinquish his share of the publishing company. Brian finally broke, and verbally agreed to give his father 100% of the publishing rights. Although no contract was signed, Murry began taking 100% of all publishing income.

On June 9, 1965, Brian received a letter from Murry reminding him that he had promised to sign over all publishing rights to his father. Murry repeatedly reminded Brian of this, even going so far as to say that Audree had witnessed this agreement, which, Murry said, had been sealed with a handshake. Brian refused to sign a contract, but Murry would not take no for an answer. He continued his verbal assault for months but eventually backed off, and Brian turned to drugs, which he had been experimenting with for some time, for solace.

In November 1969, Brian was told that Murry was going to sell Sea of Tunes to Irving Almo Publishing, a division of A&M Records. Murry believed that the Beach Boys' career was coming to an end and that their material didn't have a future outside the group's live performances. Brian confronted Murry at the Wilson home, and Murry insisted that Brian had signed over the rights. A violent argument ensued—glasses, plates, and pots were broken—but in the end Murry sold the catalog for $700,000. (Today, the songs in the catalog have an estimated worth of over $20,000,000.) Murry received the money in one lump sum and no member of the band ever saw a penny. Brian was devastated; this was akin to selling his children. He was distraught for months—the sale increased his paranoia and fueled his desire to escape into drugs and alcohol.

On September 19, 1989, Brian filed a lawsuit against A&M, Irving Almo Publishing, and the law firm that negotiated the sale of the catalog. A year before, during an audit of Almo's books, Brian's attorney had discovered some inconsistencies in the paperwork and had decided to investigate. The contracts and signatures necessary for the sale of Sea of Tunes were questionable, the law firm that had handled the sale for Irving Almo had also represented the Beach Boys at the time of the sale, and Brian Wilson's signature on the 1969 letter of transfer was a forgery. One month prior to Brian's filing of the lawsuit, the principals produced contracts that they said proved that all was indeed in order. These contracts were also problematic: some of the signatures were forgeries, and in the contracts some of the songs were stated as being transferred to Sea of Tunes before they were actually written ("Caroline, No," for instance, was written in early 1966, not in May 1962 as stated in the contract). The lawsuit was settled in 1994; Irving Almo settled with Brian Wilson for an undisclosed amount, but that company retains administration duties.

The departure from Capitol's studios and the return to Western's Studio Three gave Brian the creative freedom he needed.

But Murry's efforts to limit the money Usher might make from this collaboration did not stop here. He also found ways to prevent songs written with Usher from generating any revenue at all. As administrator of Sea of Tunes, Murry was in a position to license songs in the catalog to other artists who wanted to record them; if a song wasn't cleared by Murry, it wasn't recorded or at least wasn't released in the commercial market. And when other artists came to him to request Wilson-Usher songs from the Sea of Tunes catalog, Murry could easily suggest a song composed by Brian alone rather than the song originally requested.

By this time Murry had been able to wriggle out of his deal with the Morgans. The first royalty check for "Surfin'" was extremely small considering the number of copies that had been sold, but this wasn't completely the Morgans' fault: the distributors were slow in paying for their product and because the Morgans had used all their money to pay for pressing the records, they were out of cash. (A label can often be put out of business by a hit record. The cash paid upfront for initial pressing and promotion usually is drawn from the label's liquid assets—if the label is very small, they may put all their available cash into trying to make one song a success—and if orders are not promptly paid for, the label may not be able to press any more records to generate more revenue or even pay its other costs.) This was enough for Murry. Without consulting the Morgans, he booked the boys into Western Studios with Chuck Britz as the engineer. The group then rerecorded some of the songs recorded earlier for the Morgans, and Murry set out to make the rounds with the new demos. He was turned down by many labels, but luckily for the Beach Boys, he had a contact at Capitol: Ken Nelson, the country-western A&R man who had turned down some of Murry's songs a few years earlier. After being badgered by Murry, Nelson passed on the new Beach Boys tape to Nik Venet, Capitol's pop A&R representative. Venet was twenty-one years old, a surfer, and very much in touch with what was going on in the teen scene. By the time he reached the age of nineteen, he had already had a few hits as a producer, including one by the Lettermen. The Lettermen connection was a good starting point for Murry, and after Venet got back from a two-week vacation, Murry had a meeting with him. Unable to contain himself, he rambled on about how great his boys were. He finally managed to play "Surfin' Safari" for Venet. Eight bars in, Venet knew the song would be a hit. He told Murry he would speak to a Capitol executive about purchasing the masters, and Murry asked for a three-hundred-dollar advance per song.

The Surfer Girls

Unfortunately, little is known about the Surfer Girls other than the name of their one hit: "Draggin' Wagon." This single (and its flip side, "One Boy Tells Another") was produced by Steve Venet, brother of Nik Venet, the Capitol A&R representative who signed the Beach Boys. This record was released in March 1964 on Columbia Records. Probably because it was an obvious ripoff of the Chuck Berry sound, the composer credit is given as S. Taylor (probably one of the members of the Surfer Girls or perhaps a Columbia employee) and Chuck Berry.

Beach Boy legend has it that Murry, Brian, and Gary Usher waited in a nearby coffee shop for approximately an hour before going back up to Venet's office in the Capitol Tower and getting their answer. According to Venet and Usher, Capitol's resounding yes was not actually heard for a few days, and Murry did get his asking price, but not without almost making a huge error.

When Venet inquired about the publishing rights, Gary Usher told him they were already taken. Venet paused for a minute, surely sending Murry's blood pressure soaring. All was dead quiet until Venet said, "Okay," and made arrangements for contracts to be drawn up.

On the elevator ride down, Murry exploded in Usher's face, telling him that if he ever did something like that again, he was finished. It could have jeopardized the deal—Capitol might not have been interested if they couldn't buy the publishing rights. As things turned out, however, Murry was lucky that Usher spoke up when he did. Within just a few years, those rights were worth millions. If Murry had thought it necessary to sign over the publishing rights to get the deal, he would have done so without a moment's hesitation, and that would have benefited no one except the record company.

In an industry as full of gossip as the music business, it wasn't hard for the Morgans to find out about the impending deal with Capitol, but this didn't really bother Murry, who was angry with the Morgans over the way they had handled the royalty payments for "Surfin'." Even though this single had sold over fifty thousand copies, the group's royalty check had amounted to less than a thousand dollars. (According to the boys' contract with Guild Music, royalties were set at six cents for each copy sold, so the amount of the check should have been closer to three thousand dollars, not including income from sheet music sales or performance royalties.) This small check was Murry's excuse to get out of the deal with the Morgans, but he began shopping around a demo tape without first settling with them. Because the contract with Guild stated that anything recorded while the agreement was in effect would be the property of Guild Music, when Murry made the deal with Capitol he sold them songs he didn't own or have permission to sell. This left the Morgans in a good position to win if they chose to sue. Since they knew, however, that a court battle with Murry would have exhausted what little cash they had (and that Murry not only would bring all his energies to bear in this lawsuit and would thus easily wear the Morgans down, but also would have access to Capitol's formidable legal department), they opted to settle out of court for eighty thousand dollars. With this, their part of the Beach Boy story was written, except for a 1980s DCC (Digital Compact Classics) release of a compact disc entitled *The Beach Boys/Lost & Found 1961–1962*, which consisted of various takes of the band's early recordings with the Morgans.

Capitol Records' first Beach Boys single was released on June 4, 1962. "409" b/w "Surfin' Safari" didn't do very well in the first few weeks of release, perhaps because of the choices for A and B sides. The obvious choice would have been to put "Surfin' Safari" on the A side, but Venet thought that would garner only local airplay. Once the label started promoting the B side to radio stations across the country, the single began climbing the charts; it peaked at number fourteen for two weeks in October. New York City, which is not exactly known as a surf mecca, had the biggest order of any area.

Meanwhile, a twelve-hour studio session resulted in the Beach Boys' first album, also called *Surfin' Safari*. It took three months for the album to reach its peak at number thirty-two on the charts.

One of the earliest Beach Boys recording sessions, featuring (from left to right) Mike Love, Brian Wilson, Carl Wilson, Dennis Wilson, and David Marks.

The group also began its first tour that summer, with one personnel change. Before the Capitol contracts had been signed, Alan Jardine quit the group to return to dental school. He was replaced by David Marks, a neighbor of the Wilsons. Marks was fourteen when the group hit the road; Carl was only a year older.

The next single was the first release to feature the trademarks of the Beach Boys: the intricate harmonies, Brian's falsetto voice, and the beginning of Brian's production ideas—the placement of the increasingly intricate vocal arrangements up front, the multitrack layering of vocals and instruments, and experimental or unusual arrangements—all of which crystallized into the Beach Boys sound. Taking a cue from Chubby Checker's "Twistin' U.S.A." and using a melody similiar to Chuck Berry's "Sweet Little Sixteen," "Surfin' U.S.A." made it all the way to number three. The album of the same name was rushed out and, because of the band's increasing popularity, spent seventy-eight weeks on the charts. Compared to later albums, it was not, aside from the singles, a strong record. At the time, albums consisted of two or three single-quality songs and several filler tunes. If a group was expected to put out three or four albums per year, instrumental tracks had to be used as filler, because the group simply would not have time to write songs with vocals. The number of instrumentals on *Surfin' U.S.A.* is a clear indication that Brian and the boys were not being given enough preparation time before the recording sessions of this period. Because the Beach Boys sound was defined by the vocal arrangements, the inclusion of so many instrumentals made for a weak album.

The Astronauts

Boulder, Colorado, doesn't usually come to mind when one thinks of surf music, but RCA's release of the song "Baja," by a Boulder-area bar band called the Astronauts, helped spread the music inland and eastward. Originally known as the Stormtroopers, this band consisted of three guitarists—Bob Demmon, Rich Fifield, and Dick Sellars—bassist Stormy Patterson, and drummer Jim Gallagher. In 1962 they changed their name, and later that year Sellars was replaced by Dennis Lindsey.

The Astronauts were the only surf band who came from an inland locale.

Demmon and Gallagher's meeting with Steve Sholes at the offices of RCA Records in the spring of 1963 led to the group's involvement with surf music. During the meeting, Sholes received a call regarding the phenomenal sales of the Beach Boys' *Surfin' U.S.A.* album. Placing his hand over the mouthpiece, Sholes asked the two if the Astronauts also played surf music. Eager to get a record deal, they assured him that they did. Sholes set up an audition for the group in Boulder in three weeks. Demmon and Gallagher returned to Colorado, and the band proceeded to rehearse surf tunes eight hours a day for the next three weeks. They passed the audition and were signed to RCA.

In April 1963 the group flew to Los Angeles to record their first full-length album. *Surfin' with the Astronauts*, which contained fourteen tracks, was recorded over the course of three one-hour sessions. The group's unfamiliarity with the surf culture was evident in their naming an original song "Kuk" instead of "Kook." "Baja," an original song penned by Los Angeles songwriter-producer Lee Hazelwood, was "suggested" by Al Schmitt, the A&R man who had signed the Astronauts. This song turned out to be the group's biggest hit, spending one week on the *Billboard* charts, where it reached number ninety-four in late 1963. The album also did quite well, selling more than one million copies.

The group continued to record and tour throughout the early 1960s. They appeared in a few movies, among them *Surf Party*, and toured Japan. In 1966 the group dissolved due to the popularity of the Beatles and the war in Vietnam. The members who weren't shipped off to the war renamed themselves the Sunshineward and released a few singles, effectively ending the surf music phase of the Astronauts and the city of Boulder.

By this time, rock and roll was still less than ten years old and no one could predict with any accuracy how long any group would last. Acts came and went with such frequency that the prevailing attitude at most labels was that the wisest course of action was always to strike as fast as possible, as often as possible, filling the marketplace with as much product as could be distributed. The Beach Boys were no exception—at this time they were still considered just another surf act. Because Capitol producers couldn't know how long the group would remain popular, they followed company policy and put the boys to work at an amazing pace. The band was expected to release at least three full albums a year, tour endlessly to promote those albums, and make numerous promotional appearances (in stores, on television and the radio, and in interviews for magazines and newspapers).

Many people would have collapsed under those pressures. No matter what role one had to play—writer, producer, or touring musician—the schedule would have been too much. Brian Wilson, who was all three of these, rose to the occasion, at least for a while. Not only did he manage to do all that was required of him, but his power in the studio also grew—with each successive recording session, he was given more say, until he was eventually given full rein. This power did not come easily, however; his father berated him at every turn, and Murry's relentless criticisms eventually resulted in his being fired by the group.

Brian Wilson working the console in the late seventies. Strangely enough for such a talented and prolific composer-producer, he has only 4 percent hearing in his left ear.

One of Brian's first moves as producer was to return to Western Studios and work with Chuck Britz. At the time it was unheard of for an act to demand that they work at an outside studio, but Brian was adamant, and he sent Murry to Capitol to work it out.

"Surfer Girl," recorded in the spring of 1963, was the first single produced after the return to Western, and the difference was noticeable. The first ballad released by the group, it was also the first song recorded by Brian without any of the other Beach Boys. (Conducting solo recording sessions was to become the norm in the coming years, after Brian suffered a nervous breakdown and quit touring in order to concentrate on studio work.) "Surfer Girl" reached number seven, and its flip side, "Little Deuce Coupe," reached number fifteen. This was the last surf song the group would release as a single.

The Beach Boys at the Hollywood Bowl in November 1963, about a year before Brian stopped touring with the band.

As a songwriter, arranger, and producer, Brian was developing at an amazing rate. The success of each release was further proof that he was going in the right direction. His compositions grew more introspective and further away from fun in the sun, and his arrangements grew further and further from the band's early arrangements. The guys in the band, particularly Mike Love, felt that Brian was straying too far from the formula that had gotten them where they were.

In any case, the Beach Boys were the biggest group at Capitol—and one of the biggest in the world—until the Beatles came along. Once Capitol saw the earning potential of the Fab Four, all other artists on the label were cast into limbo, but the Beach Boys would not let themselves be forgotten. In the summer of 1964, they went on their first tour of Europe; the trip was a huge success, and the English dates were particularly noteworthy. On July 4 the Beach Boys had their first number one hit: "I Get Around." At one point in the fall of 1964, there were seven Beach Boys songs on the charts; "Fun, Fun, Fun" stalled at number five because Beatles songs occupied the top four spots.

In December 1964, the boys were scheduled for a short promotional tour of Texas. It was during the flight to Houston that Brian experienced his first nervous breakdown. There had been signs that this was going to happen—Brian had been missing shows frequently (often showing up drunk when he bothered to show up at all), and complaining of ear pain and fatigue—and Al Jardine had been brought back to fill in for Brian when necessary. Jardine's presence not only helped make up for the loss of Brian, but also enabled Murry to fire David Marks, with whom he had been warring almost constantly. Brian eventually told the rest of the band that he would no longer be able to tour with them; instead, he would spend his time in the studio. Guitarist Glen Campbell was hired in February 1965, but soon left for the stability and better pay of session work; he was replaced in April by Bruce Johnston, who—except for the years 1972 to 1978, when he left because of disagreements with then-manager Jack Rieley—has been a Beach Boy ever since.

Brian Wilson holding a mirror reflecting the rest of the Beach Boys.

The Rip Chords/Bruce and Terry

The original Rip Chords were a duo: Ernie Bringas and Phil Stewart. After the two were signed by Columbia Records, Terry Melcher and Bruce Johnston (who later joined the Beach Boys) were brought in to sing, produce, and generally oversee the band's operations. Produced by Melcher and Johnston, the band's best-known single, "Hey Little Cobra," was released in November 1963. The vocals were augmented by Arnie Marcus and Rich Rotkin.

Melcher and Johnston's recording sessions involved a rotating cast of vocalists and musicians. The performers who toured with the band also varied, and because of their busy recording schedules, Melcher and Johnston never went on the road with the Rip Chords. The Wrecking Crew, when available, were the musicians of choice in the studio.

The Rip Chords were just one of a handful of names used by the Melcher and Johnston production team. They also recorded as the Rogues and as Bruce and Terry. Presumably, the label felt that the public would buy more records if the songs were put out under different band names (apparently, the label also felt that, because of the anonymity provided by the studio, the record buyers would not catch on to the fact that these "different" bands were actually the same musicians). The record company would market records by following sales reports: Melcher and Johnston would record a song, the label would investigate which "group" was then generating the most revenue, and the record would be released under the most popular moniker. Once the popularity of a particular "group" began to wane, the label would discontinue that name and move on to one that was more popular. The record company would further deceive the public by simultaneously issuing Melcher-Johnston productions under different names.

By the time Bruce Johnston joined the Beach Boys in 1965, he had amassed an extensive discography. Prior to working with Melcher, he had recorded or produced for MGM, Capitol, and Del-Fi, among others. He also wrote a number of tunes for the Beach Boys, but his greatest songwriting credit is probably "I Write the Songs," made famous by pop star Barry Manilow. He remains an active member of the Beach Boys.

The Rip Chords were one of many sixties studio bands produced by Bruce Johnston and Terry Melcher.

Terry Melcher, the son of Doris Day, has been involved in numerous endeavors. He has produced records and television shows, and has been a fixture of the Hollywood scene since the early 1960s. His friendship with Dennis Wilson of the Beach Boys led to an audition by an aspiring folksinger named Charles Manson. Repeated efforts by Manson to interest Melcher in his music were in vain. Eventually, Manson opted for scare tactics and on August 9, 1969, sent a few members of his "family" to Melcher's house at 10050 Cielo Drive in Los Angeles. Melcher, however, was not living at the house at the time; he was leasing it to film director Roman Polanski, and the Manson Family butchered five people, including Sharon Tate, Polanski's wife. Terry Melcher has remained a presence in the music industry and continues to produce records to this day.

The Beach Boys Today, released in early 1965, was the first album Brian was able to work on without interruption. Opinions on the album are mixed but most fans and critics agree that the single "When I Grow Up to Be a Man" was a solid Beach Boys effort. By this time, Capitol again had the group working overtime—they had proven to Capitol that the Beatles were not the only money makers around—and *Summer Days (And Summer Nights!!!)* came out just a few months after *The Beach Boys Today*. Two singles from the *Summer Days* LP, "Help Me, Rhonda" and "California Girls," have remained concert staples.

Brian's increasing studio expertise, fueled by his new experiments with drugs, found him unsatisfied with the production-line mentality that pervaded the record industry. His idea to record the band in a party atmosphere was as much a break from the formula as it was a way of gaining the time he needed to fulfill his vision of the album that was in his head. The next LP, *Beach Boys Party!*, released in November 1965, was recorded in various locations over a few different sessions. Wives, friends, and pets were all present, and with the assistance of Dean Torrance (of Jan & Dean), who happened to be recording down the hall, the band recorded "Barbara Ann," which made it all the way to number two. The album spent six months on the charts, finally reaching the Top Ten in early 1966. Capitol's publicity department went so far as to distribute to record stores a million bags of potato chips with the album artwork on them.

By the time *Beach Boys Party!* was released, there were enough of the group's LPs and singles on the charts and in the stores to satisfy the bloodlust of the executives at Capitol. Since *Party!* had been recorded in only three or four sessions, there was

Brian and Hal Blaine at Western Studios in 1963. Brian frequently asked Blaine and other members of the Wrecking Crew for creative input.

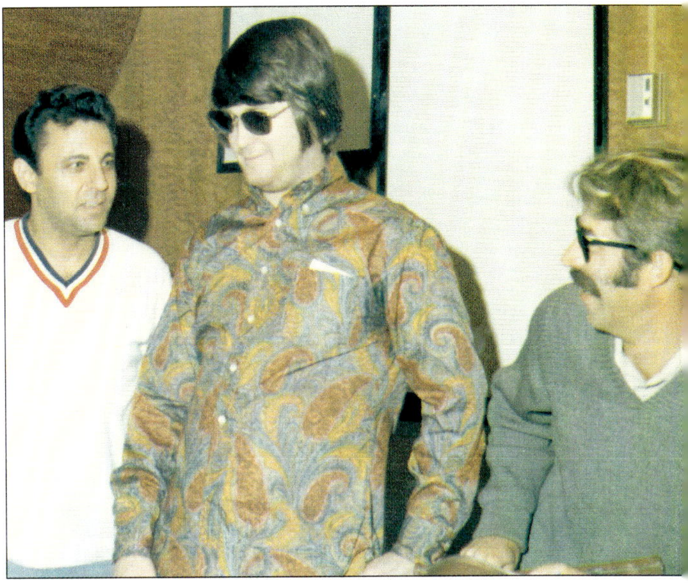

Hal Blaine (left), Brian Wilson (center) and bassist Ray Pohlman around the time of the Pet Sounds sessions.

more time for the development and production of the next record, which enabled Brian to create his masterpiece, *Pet Sounds*. This album was ahead of its time in many ways. The subject material was of a more melancholy nature; the loss of teen innocence and search for spirituality were a far cry from fun, fun, fun; and Brian sang most of the lead vocals, again using session players (the Wrecking Crew, the same group Dick Dale worked with when not using the Deltones), since the band was on the road at the time. Brian's collaboration with Tony Asher resulted in some of the most groundbreaking works in rock history, including "Wouldn't It Be Nice," "God Only Knows," and "Caroline, No." His arrangement of the traditional song "Sloop John B."—a few years earlier, Jardine had suggested that the group cover this tune, but Brian had seemed unimpressed—was a classic example of his shift in style and musical choices. Because the production of the album cost at least fifty thousand dollars (an absurdly high figure for the time) and the record lacked a "real Beach Boy" single, the executives at Capitol were less than pleased. The band was equally baffled. Now reduced to just adding their vocal parts to instrumental tracks put down by the Wrecking Crew, they were understandably apprehensive about being able to reproduce the songs onstage, and this apprehension was no secret. The powers at Capitol gave *Pet Sounds* no support and even released a greatest-hits package within a few months of the record's release, killing what momentum Brian Wilson's masterwork might have had.

Beatle Paul McCartney was said to have played the record over and over for days. He claims it was a huge influence on *Sgt. Pepper's Lonely Hearts Club Band*, and has said on numerous occasions that "God Only Knows" is the most beautiful song ever written. Brian, and a select few, realized that this was his best effort to date, and the beginning of a period of amazing creativity.

The group's next release, the single "Good Vibrations," turned out to be Brian's last great release with the Beach Boys, as well as the group's first million-selling single and their biggest hit ever.

Good Vibrations

Not satisfied with the popular and critical acclaim generated by *Pet Sounds*, Brian Wilson returned to the studio in the early summer of 1966 to begin work on what he called his "pocket symphony": the song "Good Vibrations."

The years 1962 through 1966 found Brian at his creative peak.

The song's title was inspired by Audree Wilson. When Brian was a child, she often told him that dogs barked at some people but not at others because of the "vibrations" people gave off. Brian's intent with "Good Vibrations" was to meld his newfound spirituality with his recording and producing talents to create the perfect pop song.

The sessions involved in the piecing together of the song were the talk of the music industry. In his autobiography, Brian contests the reported six-month recording time; he says that the song was created in six weeks of actual studio time, over a period of three months. The recording of the three-minute, thirty-five-second song involved twenty sessions in four different studios and was produced from ninety hours of tape. Production costs have been estimated to be anywhere from fifty to seventy-five thousand dollars, and even the lower amount was unheard of at the time. Engineer Chuck Britz manned the mixing board for all twenty sessions, and instrumentation was provided by the Wrecking Crew. For the initial sessions, about twenty musicians were used; the Beach Boys came in at the end to provide missing vocal tracks.

The song was divided into three separate sections. The editing required multiple sessions, as sections of tape were spliced together in a meticulous fashion. The instrumentation set new parameters for pop songs as Brian added sleigh bells, wind chimes, flutes, organ, harpsichord, Jew's harp, fuzz bass, harp, cello, clarinet, and a Theramin (a kind of synthesizer with a heat-sensitive "keyboard" that had been used in the soundtracks to a few horror movies of the 1940s and 1950s but was new to rock and roll).

Bruce Johnston summed up the feelings of many persons in the rock world—those involved in the creation of the song as well as those outside it—when he said, "We're gonna have either the biggest hit in the world, or the Beach Boys' career is over." But their career did not end here—the song was a tremendous hit. Released on October 10, 1966, "Good Vibrations" sold 100,000 copies a day in its first four days of release. In just a few weeks it became the biggest single of the group's career. It went to number one in the United States and England, and eventually sold more than 16,000,000 copies worldwide.

Brian Wilson in 1980, three years before his second round of therapy with psychiatrist Eugene Landy.

Brian's descent into madness picked up steam at this point. His next album, *Smile*, was never completed, though a few cuts made it onto the boxed set and various bootleg albums. The world was changing radically and the group was seen as being too out-of-touch with current events and musical trends. To try to survive, they began a series of tours and mediocre albums, but to no avail. The resurgence of the group began in the mid-1970s with *Endless Summer*—released on June 24, 1974, this collection of the group's biggest 1960s hits reached number one on October 5, 1974, and spent most of the next two and a half years on the *Billboard* charts—and continued throughout the eighties with their annual Fourth of July shows in Washington, D.C. Brian stayed in his room for most of the seventies, appearing in public only periodically; this confirmed everyone's suspicions about his mental and physical state.

The story of Brian's mental breakdown could fill a book. By the mid-sixties drugs had become rather prevalent in the rock and roll world, and Brian's abuse of LSD and marijuana probably contributed to his eventual collapse. By the early 1970s, he was no longer involved in the production of the group's material and was spending most of his time in bed. He continued to ingest huge quantities of cocaine, heroin, alcohol, and other drugs, and he put on a great deal of weight. He stopped bathing—he was afraid that snakes or fire would come out of his showerhead if he turned the water on—and was often seen wandering around his Bel Air neighborhood in a bathrobe and pajamas.

By 1975 Brian's wife, Marilyn (the two had been married in late 1964), had lost all patience with Brian. He had been in need of psychiatric care for some time, but no one had really been willing to face this issue. Eugene Landy's unorthodox (for a psychiatrist) appearance—jeans, boots, and unkempt hair—appealed to Marilyn, and, realizing that Brian wouldn't respond well to a "regular" doctor, she hired Landy. To say that Landy's methods were unusual is an understatement. First and foremost, he stated that he must be allowed complete control over Brian's life. He banished all of Brian's drug buddies, put a lock on the refrigerator, and after a few months had Brian on a strict regimen of diet, exercise, and productive activity.

Eugene Landy (left) with a stable and seemingly happy Brian Wilson in 1991.

The Beach Boys were eager to have their songwriter-producer back and they pushed for his return. Landy warned them that Brian needed to get a little more established within himself before he could deal with them, but their selfish behavior eventually forced Landy out of the picture in December 1976.

With Landy's departure, Brian quickly relapsed into his old behavior, and his weight eventually soared from 180 to 340 pounds. He again took to his bed, and drugs became a bigger problem than before. Eventually, the rest of the group had no choice but to bring Landy back into the picture. It took Landy and the group six months to get Brian to again submit to the doctor's rigorous demands, but with his money being withheld and the band firing him on November 5, 1982 (in an effort to get him to straighten out), he had few options. Landy had him checked into a hospital in January 1983 and flown to Hawaii later that month. This time, the therapy stuck, and Brian went back to work, recording two solo albums and appearing with the group now and again.

Landy's twenty-four-hour therapy was questioned by many in the Beach Boys camp as well as by many in the medical field. The pressure to dissolve the formal doctor-patient relationship led to the pressing of charges by the California board of psychiatric practice. In January 1988 Landy and Brian terminated their doctor-patient relationship, agreeing that they would instead work as cowriters and friends, with Landy acting as Brian's manager. The Beach Boys, however, remained unsatisfied, and their efforts to separate Brian and Landy resulted in an unsuccessful attempt to have a conservator attached to Brian (that is, they wanted to choose someone—preferably a relative—to manage Brian's personal and financial affairs). In order to avoid this, Brian and Landy had to sever all ties, proving that Brian was capable of managing his own affairs and that he wasn't reliant upon and had not been brainwashed by Landy. In the spring of 1991, the two signed a mutual-consent separation agreement, officially ending their relationship.

Dennis Wilson in Los Angeles in 1971, twelve years before his death by drowning.

But Brian was not the only Beach Boy mired in tragedy. Dennis Wilson's bouts with cocaine and booze eventually led to his death by drowning in a California harbor just after Christmas in 1983. Though grieving, the rest of the group went on without him; in 1988 they had a number one hit with "Kokomo," their first since "Good Vibrations" twenty-two years earlier.

Surfing

The sport of surfing was said to have originated in the Polynesian Islands, though there is evidence of the Incas having surfed off the coast of Lima, Peru. Captain James Cook reported seeing surfers on his visit to the Hawaiian Islands in 1778. The missionaries who followed Cook convinced the natives that surfing should be discouraged, and by the beginning of the twentieth century the sport had almost died out in the Islands.

George Freeth, who surfed Redondo Beach in 1907, has the distinction of being the first recorded surfer on the California coast. Duke Kahanamoku, an Olympic swimming star in the 1912 and 1920 Games, helped to bring attention to the sport when he stopped in California with his surfboard on the way to the 1912 Games.

In the beginning, surfboards were extremely heavy—upwards of a hundred pounds—and very long—eleven to fourteen feet in average length. Californians Tom Blake and Bob Simmons's work with balsa wood boards covered in fiberglass resulted in boards that were much less cumbersome, an appealing factor for women and children. By the 1950s, the sport had exploded in popularity. Residents of Australia, Hawaii, and both coasts of the United States were flocking to the beaches. Clubs were organized and professional tour circuits were initiated. Surfing even moved inland to pools with man-made waves and to some of the larger bodies of water that had some tidal activity.

Surfing is as popular today as ever. Basic surfing style has evolved from a passive "go where the wave takes you" approach to a more aggressive, master-the-ocean one. With boards now ranging from five feet to ten feet in length, the maneuverability of surfers has increased, allowing them to attack the wave, cutting back into the curl repeatedly. Some of the more famous surfing spots are Sunset, the Banzai Pipeline, and Waimea Bay, on the north shore of Hawaii; Waikiki and Ala Moana on the south shore of Oahu; Santa Cruz and Carmel, near San Francisco; and Rincon, Redondo Beach, Malibu, Huntington Beach, and Laguna Beach, near Los Angeles. The coasts of Africa, Australia, and South America also boast hundreds of spots frequented by surfers.

Surf Terminology

Surfing and surf music might seem to have a language all their own. While some of the terms—for example, "wipeout" and "ding"—have entered the mainstream, others remain indigenous to the surf-skateboard world. The following is a brief glossary of surfing words and phrases:

Baggies: Oversized swim trunks worn by younger surfers.

Bail out: A planned escape from a surfboard to avoid being wiped out by an oncoming wave.

Big gun: A surfboard eleven feet or more in length. Big guns are used to ride large waves; their size gives the surfer more stability but little maneuverability.

Bottom turn: A wide turn made at the bottom of or well below the crest of a wave.

Curl: The section of the wave that is spilling over and breaking.

Cut back: To turn the surfboard back into the breaking part of the wave.

Ding: A hole or gouge in the surface of a surfboard; also, an injury suffered by a surfer.

Drop in: To ride down the face of a wave to gain speed.

Face: The unbroken front of a wave.

Goofy-foot: A surfer who rides with his right foot forward. (Most surfers ride with the left foot forward.)

Gremlin (or Gremmie): A novice surfer whose inexperience is obvious to other surfers; usually applied to one who is too rowdy for other surfers in the area.

Hang ten: To place the toes over the front or extreme forward portion of a surfboard.

Hot-dogging: Showy surfing performed by experienced surfers; usually involves tricks and stunts rather than simple wave riding.

Kick out: To push the tail of the board down to lift and turn the nose over the top of a wave.

Pearl: When the nose of a surfboard drops enough to slow or stop the board.

Rail: The rounded edge of a surfboard.

Set: A group of waves coming in a short period of time.

Shooting the curl: Riding the wave at the curl, hopefully with a tube forming around the surfer.

Soup: The foamy part of a wave; the whitewater.

Surfari: A trip made by surfers in search of good waves.

Swells: A series of unbroken waves moving in similar fashion and having a similar shape and size.

Tube: The hollowed-out channel of water at the crest of a wave.

Wipeout: A fall from a surfboard.

Woody: The wooden-bodied station wagons used by surfers to haul their boards to the beach.

Jan & Dean

Jan Berry (1941–) and Dean Torrance (1940–) were high school classmates in Los Angeles in the late fifties. Their earliest recording efforts were made in Jan's garage. After Dean's enlistment in the army ended the first phase of their collaboration, Jan released a series of singles with Arnie Ginsburg on Arwin Records; one of these, a song called "Jennie Lee," made the Top Ten in May 1958.

Jan Berry (left) and Dean Torrance began as a pop duo, but they found their greatest success as a surf band.

In 1959 Dean returned from the army and resumed recording with Jan. On the strength of their homemade demo tapes, they got a deal with Dore Records, owned by Herb Alpert and Lou Adler. (Alpert would later found A&M Records with Jerry Moss, as well as play trumpet and lead the Tijuana Brass. Adler was a producer who also worked with the Mamas and the Papas, the Turtles, and Carole King, among others.) While with Dore, Jan & Dean had a Top Ten hit with "Baby Talk." A disagreement over the song "Heart and Soul" caused Adler to take the group to Liberty Records. Liberty liked Jan & Dean, but passed on the song. Adler, however, was convinced that the song had great potential, and he approached Challenge Records, which signed the band to a two-single deal, and "Heart and Soul" was finally released. The group fulfilled its contractual obligation to Challenge and signed with Liberty in late 1961.

Independent Labels

Within the music industry there are two groups of record labels: the "majors" and the "indies." The majors today consist of five organizations: BMG (Bertelsmann Music Group), CEMA (owned by Capitol/EMI), Sony, WEA (Warner Brothers, Elektra, and Atlantic), and PGD (Polygram Distribution). These companies manage their own distribution, and the business they do makes up the majority of sales in the industry. The indies, which often support only a few artists each, are distributed via a network of regional and national companies. Many acts develop a catalog of work and a steady following on an independent label before signing with a major label. In cases where an act is dropped by a major due to lack of sales, that act is sometimes signed by an indie. This is beneficial for an artist because he or she receives greater support from a smaller label; in a small company that has little operating capital, the investment is greater than in a large company and the label therefore makes greater efforts to ensure a return on each investment.

With the exception of a few acts (for example, the Beach Boys and Dick Dale), most of the surf bands were signed to independent labels, which were usually formed to release a certain artist's material; this was the best promotion and distribution option for those groups who weren't ready for the major recording companies or who had no access to the bigger labels.

Many of the indies that supported surf music had only one act on their roster, and this often led to those labels having very short lives. Inexperienced label owners and operators were often victimized by distributors and retailers. A label might use all of its assets to pay for pressing a record, only to be shortchanged when a distributor handed the company an inaccurate inventory report. When dealing with recalcitrant distributors, one of the few ways a label could try to force payment was by holding up a new release until the distributor paid for records already sold. If an act was hot, the label usually was paid; if not, the label could turn to other regional distributors and accept the loss. If a record did not sell very well, returns could result in little or no profit—and sometimes even substantial losses—on that song. Many labels folded with boxes of unsold records sitting in warehouses around the country. The indies that were successful achieved that success through diligent bookkeeping, the maintenance of an adequate cash flow through slow times, and a salable catalog.

Today, independent labels are stronger than ever. With the success of MTV and college radio, more and more acts are finding alternate avenues of exposure. With the advent of Soundscan (a method of recording sales electronically by scanning a product's bar code, the small pattern of bars and numbers found somewhere on the packaging of most products), accuracy in sales reports has been ensured. In the past, distributors and retailers were often given free products, cash, tickets to shows, or other "rewards" if they would report that a certain release had sold more copies than it actually had. Obviously, the smaller labels couldn't afford this kind of "reporting," and the majors therefore consistently received the top spots on all the playlists. The new method proves what those in the industry have known all along: that there are many indies selling on a par with the majors. While this has convinced the majors of the wisdom of buying up those independents who have achieved success on their own, not all indies succumb to the lure of bigger dollars offered by the majors; many retain their independent status in an effort to keep the grassroots attitude and achievements alive.

Jan & Dean's first release on Liberty Records was "A Sunday Kind of Love." Similiar in style to "Heart and Soul," the song only reached number ninety-five on the *Billboard* charts. The follow-up song was called "Tennessee," and though it reached number sixty-nine, it was still in the style of the previous two releases. A few more singles were recorded before "Linda" was released at the end of 1962. Their best showing on Liberty to date, this single peaked at number twenty-eight.

Jan & Dean's early releases on Liberty suffered from a formulaic surf-tune approach, primarily because the songs were chosen by the production team, not the musicians. After Jan Berry was given the opportunity to choose and produce the duo's material, in late 1962 or early 1963, Jan & Dean found their niche. It was also in early 1963 that Brian Wilson, the leader of the Beach Boys, entered the picture. The Beach Boys had been the opening act for Jan & Dean on a few occasions and Brian had become friendly with the headliners. Their decision to collaborate resulted in a number-one record, the first for Jan & Dean and for Brian Wilson (the Beach Boys recorded the song some time later, but their version didn't go to number one).

The promotion of Jan Berry (at the piano) to the producer's chair colidified Jan & Dean's trademark sound.

One afternoon in early 1963, Brian stopped by to visit Jan & Dean. As they sat at the piano, Brian played a new composition entitled "Surfin' U.S.A." Jan liked the tune and asked if he and Dean could record it. Brian said that he was planning to use this song for a Beach Boys record, but he had written another, "Surf City," which he was willing to let the duo record. He also gave Jan permission to finish writing the lyrics, and sang backing vocals for Jan & Dean's recording of the tune. In July 1963 the song reached number one on the *Billboard* pop chart. They finished out the year with "Drag City," which was more or less a new version of "Surf City" in which the beaches mentioned in the song were changed to cars and streets.

The cover to the "Drag City" single.

The Guitar Ramblers

Due to the lack of documentation about this era, there is little information available on the Guitar Ramblers. It is known that they were a group of studio musicians and that they were produced by Jim Herbert, under the direction of Jack Marshall. The album *Happy, Youthful Sounds*, which included the hit single "Surf Beat," was released by Columbia Records in October 1963.

Before the mid-sixties it had been rare for an artist to release two chart-quality songs on the same single. Record labels usually reserved the B side of a single for a song that didn't make it as an album cut or just wasn't considered single material. Artists who would disagree with label management over this policy were rare. In the sixties, however, there arose a new kind of musician, who felt that an entire album should consist of more than just a few singles and seven or eight filler tracks. The Beatles, the Rolling Stones, and the Beach Boys were some of the first artists to see rock as an art form rather than as disposable entertainment, and Jan Berry's diligent studio efforts were certainly on par with those of his peers. As a result, Jan & Dean released quite a few 45s on which both the A and B sides charted.

"Dead Man's Curve" b/w "New Girl In School" was released in February 1964. The artwork on the sleeve was proof that both Liberty Records and Jan & Dean intended that both songs should be treated as charting material. (Normally, the song on the A side of a single is listed in bigger type and the artwork on that side of

A notorious perfectionist in the studio, Jan (shown here with engineer Bones Howel at the console) treated every song as a potential single.

the sleeve has more interesting photos and illustrations; for this single, the type and artistic treatments were similar for both songs.) The logic was that if "Dead Man's Curve" did not appeal to listeners (the song is about drag races held on the strip of road preceding the sharp turn called "Dead Man's Curve"), the DJs could play the flip side. Unlike most singles of the period, this record consisted of rerecorded (or at least remixed) versions of the album cuts. Because Liberty, who had wanted to capitalize on the success of the "Drag City" single by releasing an album of the same name, had forced the band to rush the production of this new album, the songs were recorded under less-than-desirable conditions, which meant that they were of lower quality than the boys would have liked. For a perfectionist like Jan Berry, this was a travesty; he would have liked more time to experiment with the arrangements and the mixing. Berry and Torrance were both dissatisfied with the album and, believing that these two songs in particular had great single potential, they returned to the studio. Their belief that they could improve on the originals paid off when both tunes charted, within three weeks of each other; "Dead Man's Curve" reached number eight and "New Girl in School" went to number thirty-seven. Brian Wilson and his current writing partner, Roger Christian, were listed as cowriters.

"The Little Old Lady From Pasadena," "Ride the Wild Surf," "Sidewalk Surfin'," and "The Anaheim, Azusa, & Cucamonga Sewing Circle, Book Review and Timing Association" were released in 1964. *The T.A.M.I. Show (The Teenage Awards Music International Show)*, which starred the Rolling Stones, James Brown, the Supremes, Chuck Berry, Marvin Gaye, the Beach Boys, and numerous other rock and roll superstars of the time, was filmed at the end of that year. Jan & Dean were chosen as the hosts, and they sang the theme song, "(Here They Come) From All Over the World." The movie has become a must-see for any fan of rock and roll.

"The Little Old Lady from Pasadena" was just one of Jan & Dean's many 1964 releases.

The ballads released in 1965 showed a change of direction for Jan & Dean. They were starting to move away from surf material and into more conceptual work.

A bit of not-so-subtle advertising for Dodge from the "Sidewalk Surfin'" sleeve.

Among this work was the album *Jan & Dean Meet Batman*. The television show *Batman*, which was quite popular at this time, spawned many a takeoff LP; there were comedy albums, rock recordings, and releases featuring various versions of the show's theme music. The Jan & Dean release featured a single entitled "Batman," which would turn out to be the duo's last.

In 1966 "Dead Man's Curve" again made the duo famous. This time, however, it was the place, not the song, that became associated with Jan & Dean—it was the site of Jan Berry's near-fatal car accident. After this horrible accident, he remained in a coma for a month. Once he came out of the coma, he began intensive therapy: he had to relearn to speak, eat, and walk; even the most basic motor functions were beyond him.

Liberty took advantage of the free press generated by Jan's misfortune and released a few more singles, even rereleasing "New Girl in School." While Jan began his therapy, Dean continued to record Jan & Dean material, which was released both on Columbia and on Jan & Dean's own label, J&D Records. He also founded Kittyhawk Graphics and created quite a few album covers (including the recent Beach Boys boxed set). The Beach Boys invited Jan & Dean to open for them on the 1978 tour. The album created from recordings made during this tour was panned by critics and fans alike. To this day, Jan continues to suffer from slight aphasia (a loss of the ability to speak or understand speech) and to experience some loss of control on his right side. Dean continues to do graphic work. The 1978 movie *Dead Man's Curve* starred Richard Hatch as Jan and Bruce Davison as Dean.

Skateboards

Another offshoot of the surfing craze was the skateboard. Riding a skateboard was as close to surfing as many landlocked fans were going to get.

The early models were usually twelve to eighteen inches long with clay or steel wheels. The ride was anything but smooth, as every pebble and crack in the sidewalk could be felt. The suspension unit, or "truck," allowed for little or no maneuverability; it was not until substantial modifications were made to this design that tricks that are basic to almost every skateboarder today were developed. The invention of the polyurethane wheel in the mid-1970s reintroduced the skateboard to a new generation of sidewalk surfers, as well as the skeptical skaters from ten years earlier. Rubber bushings (cushions between the truck base and the axle that give the skater the ability to direct the board's direction by shifting his or her weight) were added to the truck, and axles were modified to withstand severe punishment. The deck (the board itself) was lengthened and made wider, creating the opportunity for riders to take their boards into uncharted terrain, including empty swimming pools, concrete waterways, and circular cement pipeways that measured thirty feet in diameter.

Every fad has to have a soundtrack, and the skateboard craze of the 1960s was no exception. The most successful exploiters of the trend were Jan & Dean. Their single "Sidewalk Surfin'" reached number twenty-five on the *Billboard* charts at the end of 1964. This song used the melody from the Beach Boys' "Catch a Wave" and was cowritten by Brian Wilson and Roger Christian (Brian's collaborator at the time). Jan & Dean also released the two-part song "Skateboarding" (with part one on one album and part two on the next).

Most of the songs about skateboarding followed this formula: using an established melody from a hit surf song, 1) lament the lack of waves, 2) grab your board, and 3) use surf terminology, substituting inland locations for California references.

The Bel-Airs

The Bel-airs were formed in 1959 as a duo consisting of two high school freshmen, Paul Johnson (1947–) and Eddie Bertrand (1947?–). After meeting on a school bus, these two young men spent the next few months learning their favorite songs. They would spend the after-school hours teaching each other various patterns and making up their own songs. One of these, "Mr. Moto," later became their biggest hit.

Eddie Bertrand (left) and Paul Johnson, circa 1960.

After a few months of performing at local country clubs and UCLA frat parties, they decided to add a drummer and Richard Delvy, a school chum of Johnson's older sister, was asked to join the group. As it turned out, Delvy had no idea how to play rock and roll—he played in the high school dance band and had never played rock music—but Johnson and Bertrand decided to keep him anyway. After endless nights of playing rock records for Richard, they added a sax player: Chaz Stewart, who had played clarinet in the same dance band that Delvy played drums for. Stewart's knowledge of rock and roll was at about the same level as Delvy's, so the two founders had to teach him about rock music as well as how to play the sax. Later, Jim Roberts, a friend of Delvy, joined as the piano player, but he was mostly a studio player and rarely appeared at the band's shows.

The band played regularly for audiences at schools and rented halls throughout the summer of 1961. At the same time, Richard Delvy organized the band's first recording session. He booked the group for an hour at Liberty Recording Studios on Sunset Boulevard in Hollywood, where they cut five songs: "Mr. Moto," "Vampire," "Little Brown Jug," "Three Blind Mice Make It to Santa's Village," and "Whiplash" (later renamed "Kamikaze"). The total cost of the session, including tape and demo vinyl, was thirty-two dollars.

The band took their demo to various record labels in the area, looking for a deal. Art Labo of Original Sound offered to put out the record, but the band felt that the royalty rate he offered was too low. The next label to express interest was Candix Records. One of the current hits on this label was "Underwater" by the Frogmen; hoping to capitalize on the success of this record, Candix management asked the Bel-airs if they wanted to become the Frogmen. The band's tunes would be released under the Frogmen moniker and would step onto the national charts. The Bel-airs didn't go for it.

A few more labels passed on the demo before Arvee offered the group the then-going rate of three cents per single sold. The band accepted. The A&R man at Arvee, Sonny Bono (of Sonny and Cher), took their master tape and remixed it. "Mr. Moto" b/w "Little Brown Jug," released in the summer of 1961, was the group's first single. The band was disappointed with Arvee's promotional efforts, so they went about booking halls and promoting themselves.

The first place they booked was a local Knights of Columbus hall. By the second weekend, they were turning kids away and had to move to a bigger space. The next venue was the Eagle Hall in Redondo Beach. When more than a thousand kids showed up, the owners feared that there would be extensive damage and told the band to book its next show elsewhere. The band booked one show at the Hermosa Biltmore Hotel, which had a large ballroom on the second floor, and fifteen hundred kids showed up. The Surfer's Stomp was the dance of choice, and when the kids started dancing, the band members thought the floor might cave in.

Drummer, producer, and soon-to-be entrepeneur Richard Delvy, flanked by Sonny Bono (then an A&R representative for Arvee Records) and Cher.

When the summer of 1961 ended, the band went back to school. Through the band's efforts, the local L.A. radio stations started giving "Mr. Moto" a great deal more airplay than they had at first. Around the same time, the band started having arguments among themselves. Richard Delvy, who had assumed responsibility for the business end of the group, finally got fed up and left, later starting a new band, the Challengers. He was replaced by former Mouseketeer Dick Dodd, who had learned how to play drums on a snare sold to him by Annette Funicello.

The Bel-airs in 1961 (left to right): Eddie Bertrand, Richard Delvy, Chaz Stewart, Jim Roberts, Paul Johnson.

With their new drummer, the Bel-airs started appearing on local television shows including those hosted by Lloyd Thaxton, Sam Riddle, Wink Martindale, and Bob Eubanks. Because this circuit of shows was so small, members of different groups commonly ran into one another. It was through these television appearances that Paul Johnson became friends with the Beach Boys. When Al Jardine left the Beach Boys to return to school, Johnson was asked to join the band in his place; he declined, and David Marks took the position.

The band kept returning to the studio, but very little of what was recorded saw the light of day. Two of the songs, "Volcanic Action" and "Runaway," were released, but the band was not happy with Arvee's decision to remove the reverb on Eddie Bertrand's guitar. He was becoming quite interested in the direction Dick Dale was taking with his guitar sound and wanted the Bel-airs to go the same way. Bertrand and Dodd wanted the new direction, but Paul and the rest wanted to keep working in the same style. As a result, Eddie and Dick left to form Eddie & The Showmen. With his new band, the Challengers, Richard Delvy recorded "Volcanic Action," which he renamed "Tidal Wave," and released it on *Challengers Around the World*; he failed to give Bertrand the writer's credit.

Prior to Bertrand and Dodd's departure, the Bel-airs had become the house band at a club in Redondo Beach that had been named after them. After the two left, they were replaced by Steve Lotto on bass and George Dumas on drums. Aside from the clubs, nothing was happening for the band—no records, no press, no tours outside the local area. Infighting became a hobby for the band, and in 1963 they agreed to dissolve the group. Paul Johnson went on to form other bands, the last of which was known as Paul Johnson and the Hepcats.

For many fans, the Bel-airs were the ideal band to copy. The former members went on to form their own successful groups, and most of these remain active in the music business to this day. The fact that the members of the Bel-airs were all around the age of fifteen at the height of the group's popularity attests to the attitude prevalent at most of the labels: make a fast buck off the kids before their popularity fades. Or before they take a business course!

THE CHALLENGERS

The Challengers were formed in 1961 after Richard Delvy left the Bel-airs because of disagreements regarding his managerial fee. As manager of the Bel-airs (as well as their drummer), he had felt he deserved a bigger cut of the money, which wasn't a problem until the money actually started coming in.

With a hit single, "Mr. Moto," in his repertoire, Delvy had no difficulty in gathering another band around him. The first to come aboard was Randy Nauert, who had sat in as bassist for the Bel-airs on a few occasions. Glenn Gray, a guitarist from Detroit, was next to join. The roster of the original Challengers was made complete with the addition of Don Smoker (a.k.a. Landis) on guitar, Jim Roberts (formerly of the Bel-airs) on piano, and both Jerry Brown (previously with Dick Dale & His Del-tones) and Nick Hefner, who stayed around for only two albums, on sax.

With Paul Johnson moonlighting as their writer, the Challengers started renting halls and playing high school hops. They also convinced Jack Lewerke of West Coast Record Sales to put up the money to make a record. The instrumental tracks were all recorded on the first night, in about three and a half hours. The following night, the band attempted to add the vocal tracks, but Glenn Gray's efforts didn't satisfy the group; the remaining vocal ideas were shelved and the album was released as an instrumental. The band continued exploring the surf sound, and the first of many surf clubs in the area began meeting in Nauert's garage. This club became known as Haggerty's Surfing Club; the meetings were essentially jam sessions in which the band provided soundtracks for home movies of surfers and surf scenes.

The Challengers, circa 1964. Back, left to right: Ed Fournier, Richard Delvy, Art Fisher. Front, left to right: Phil Pruden, Randy Nauert.

The Surfaris

If there were one song that could be considered "the" surf song—the classic example of the genre—it would probably be "Wipe Out," by the Surfaris. Certainly no other song from the genre has been recorded or performed as often. Its frequent use in television advertisements and movie soundtracks has helped keep surf music alive in the minds of many who would otherwise know little or nothing about the genre.

The Surfaris, circa 1963 (left to right): Jim Fuller, Pat Connolly, Ron Wilson, Jim Pash, Bob Berryhill.

A talent show in 1961 was the turning point for the future members of the Surfaris. Bob Berryhill played Duane Eddy's "Rebel Rouser"; Jim Fuller and Pat Connolly played after him. A few months later, when the latter two (Fuller as guitarist and Connolly as bassist) started putting their band together, they remembered Berryhill and asked him to join the group as second guitarist. They later recruited drummer Ron Wilson and, within a couple of months, twelve-year-old saxophonist Jim Pash.

The recording of "Wipe Out" and "Surfer Joe" came about after Wilson told the others about a dream he had had about a song. The group booked time at Pal Recording Studio, opting for the $12.50 per hour mono session instead of the extravagant $15 per hour stereo session. Pash couldn't make the session as he had to help his father in the family business that day. "Wipe Out" was written in the studio; it was a combination of a melody created by Fuller and a sped-up version of the boys' high school marching band cadence as played by Wilson. The idea of adding breaking boards and the laugh (contributed by manager Dale Smallin) were engineer/studio owner Paul Buff's idea. On close examination of the song, one notices that the snare drum drops out near the end. This is because Wilson lost a stick partway through and improvised on the high hat for the duration. Not wanting to invest another $12.50, the group approved the version as was, and began making the rounds to label representatives. The song was eventually released on DFS (Dave Smallin's label), and the initial pressing consisted of two thousand copies, most of which were given away or sold at dances.

Richard Delvy (of Bel-airs and Challengers fame), who by this time had become a well-known Los Angeles–area producer, brought the group to the attention of John Marascolo, owner of Princess Records, who signed a deal with Smallin for the pressing rights of the single for a two-hundred-dollar cash advance. The four writers of

"Wipe Out" then signed over the publishing rights for one dollar (though they gave away ownership of the publishing rights, they still received royalties as the original performers).

Marascolo was sufficiently pleased with the sales of the single that he struck a deal with Dot Records for the national distribution rights. Apparently, the owners of the labels didn't feel that it was necessary to maintain any sense of legality or decency—the signees on the contract weren't Fuller, Berryhill, Connolly, and Wilson (the Surfaris), but Delvy, Nauert, Smoker, and Frundel (the Challengers).

But the group's difficulties did not end there; the Surfaris soon encountered more stumbling blocks. Their first full-length release on Dot contained only two songs actually recorded by the Surfaris; the rest were rerecorded by session players brought in by producer Richard Delvy. The fact that the band members were still in high school limited their live performances to the Orange County area. They continued playing dances and shows while lawyers fought their various cases in court. They recorded quite a few more songs for release on Decca; the most well known of these is probably "Point Panic."

"Hit City '64," released in March 1964, is not to be confused with the Gary Usher produced "Hit City '65," which came out the following April.

The group officially disbanded in 1966, though they continued to perform in various incarnations at record conventions and nightclubs. "Wipe Out" has been reissued on a slew of compilation albums, and has been rerecorded on numerous occasions.

In November 1962, shortly after he created Vault Records, Lewerke released "Surf Beat," of which 200,000 copies were eventually sold. (This was far and away the most copies sold of any record in the history of the genre.) Subsequently, a few of the Challengers went back into World Pacific Studios and cut a few tunes, which were released in January 1963 as *The De-Fenders Play the Big Ones* on World Pacific Records.

Because "Surf Beat" was successful, the Challengers started getting better gigs: the Show of Shows at the Los Angeles Sports Arena (with the Beach Boys, among others), the Teen-Age Fair in Hollywood, the television show *Celebrity Party* (with Dick Dale & His Del-tones), and the obligatory movie spot in *For Those Who Think Young*.

After the release of their second album, *Surfin' with the Challengers*, in April 1963, changes were made in personnel. Jerry Brown, Glenn Gray, Don Landis, and Jim Roberts all left (Roberts abandoned the rock world to work as organist at the local ice skating rink, a position that he felt had greater job security than playing for a rock and roll band). They were replaced by Phil Pruden, Art Fisher, Ed Fournier, and Raul Matute, respectively. Guitarist Jim Tucker also auditioned at this time; he was rejected by the Challengers, but later joined the Crossfires.

The Chantays

Next to "Wipe Out," the most recorded surf tune is probably "Pipeline," of which there are more than one hundred versions to date. A version by Dick Dale and Stevie Ray Vaughan was nominated for a Grammy in 1988, and artists as varied as Lawrence Welk and Johnny Thunders have covered this song on records and in movies.

The original Chantays, circa 1962 (left to right): Jim Frias, Rob Marshall, Bob Spickard, Bob Welch, Brian Carman, Warren Waters.

"Pipeline" was originally recorded by a group called the Chantays, made up of cofounders Bob Spickard and Brian Carman (both of whom played guitar), Bob Welch (drums), Rob Marshall (piano), and Warren Waters (bass). Written by Spickard and Carman in 1962, the song was first entitled "44 Magnum," then changed to "Liberty's Whip." The songwriters settled on the title "Pipeline" after they saw a surf movie that featured that legendary Hawaiian surf spot.

The band's performance at a southern California vacation spot in the summer of 1962 caught the attention of local DJ Jack Sands, who booked the band into a studio to record two songs: "Pipeline" and "Move It." Sands took the demo made from this session to various labels in the Los Angeles area before finally striking a deal with Downey Records, whose only stipulation was that the group rerecord the song. The new version of the song was almost identical to the original, except that it was in stereo. Downey released the single in December 1962, with "Move It" as the A side and "Pipeline" as the B. Although "Move It" reached number fifty-seven on KFXM, Riverside, California, it wasn't doing as well as the group and the label had hoped. Fortunately for everyone involved, one of the KFXM DJs began playing the flip side. "Pipeline" quickly vaulted up the charts to number sixteen. It reached number three in Los Angeles by March 1963 and number four on the *Billboard* charts in May of the same year. By this time, the group had recorded and released an album, also called *Pipeline*, that also charted on KFXM, reaching number one in April of that year. A second album, *Two Sides of the Chantays*, featuring vocal tracks as well as instrumentals, was released at the end of 1963.

In the spring of 1964, the band began to drift apart. Bob Welch, who left the group just prior to a Hawaiian tour, was replaced by Steve Cahn, son of Broadway lyricist Sammy Cahn and a friend of the band. After the Chantays returned from Hawaii, the group disbanded, though some of them continued to record, under other names and as the Chantays. Periodically, the original members got together in Spickard's living room for informal jam sessions. In 1981 a few of the members resurfaced as the Chantays, and they continue to perform to this day, with Welch, Spickard, and Carman being backed by various musicians.

The Challengers in a relaxed moment in 1964.

For the third album, *The Challengers On the Move: Surfing Around the World*, which was released in July 1963, Richard Delvy started bringing in session players like Herb Alpert and Hal Blaine, who played drums on the title track to the fourth album, *K-39*, which was released in August 1964. With Delvy's production ideas getting more elaborate, the band was finding it harder to reproduce the songs onstage.

Delvy's use of session players on 1963's The Challengers on the Move, as well as on later albums, angered the other Challengers.

By 1965 most bands had been displaced on (or entirely knocked off) the charts by the Beatles. The Challengers, however, were one of the lucky few to still have anything resembling a career. They became the house band on the local television show *Surf's Up*, hosted by Stan Richards, and established a new routine: they would tape a show in the afternoon, then race to another venue for a live performance that evening. They also became regulars on *American Bandstand*, which they appeared on more than fifty times. They did shows with the Rolling Stones, the Byrds, the Animals, the Jefferson Airplane, Jerry Lee Lewis, and Chuck Berry. In 1965 they toured Hawaii twice and performed on the Grammy Awards Show, for which they were chosen over the Beach Boys and the Ventures.

Randy Nauert's dislike for Delvy's production style, and his distaste for the drug scene that was then springing up, led to his leaving the band and heading to Europe in 1966. He wanted to study music in various foreign locales, and he visited thirty-three countries in the next few years. Buzz Carre, who was originally with a band called the Baymen, filled in for Nauert on the remaining gigs, including the Challengers' final tour, which took them to Peru. The Challengers have reunited twice in past years, in 1973 at the First International Surfers' Stomp (along with Dick Dale, Jan & Dean, the Marketts, the Surfaris, and others) and in 1975 at Magic Mountain (with Dale, the Rumblers, and the Surfaris). The Challengers were a prolific group, in surf music terms, and their songs appear on a number of surf compilations.

Kathy Marshall (1949–   ), Queen of the Surf Guitar

Kathy Marshall, pictured here in 1963, shared the stage with many top surf acts, including Dick Dale.

Kathy Marshall was only thirteen years old when she made her debut with the Blazers at her sister's ninth-grade graduation party. She had been playing guitar for approximately a year and a half when she got up to play "Pipeline." Apparently quite impressed with her performance that evening, the group's manager asked her to appear with the Blazers in some shows at local venues.

Kathy and the Blazers got the enviable spot of playing between Eddie & the Showmen's sets at the Retail Clerk's Hall. This led to regular performances with the Showmen, in which Kathy and Eddie would alternate guitar solos onstage.

For the next few years, Kathy continued playing with the Blazers and various other bands from the area, including the Crossfires, but she was never featured on any album. After leaving the Showmen in 1965, Kathy Marshall did a few more shows at Disneyland before retiring from touring to concentrate on graduating from high school.

The two songs she recorded, which were written for her by Don Wilson and Mel Taylor of the Ventures, were never released. Bootleg copies of the acetate do exist, but they are extremely hard to find.

Hot Rods

Without a car, it is almost impossible to get anywhere in southern California. To many teenagers, especially those who didn't surf, a car was *the* most important purchase they would make before going off to college. Owning the right car could save a lot of guys from dateless Friday nights.

A car was also important because without one it was almost impossible to get yourself and your surfboard to the water. The most common cars for surfers were station wagons and hearses. Many bands used the same vehicles to haul their equipment from one show to another.

Drag races were extremely popular with teenagers and younger adults. Although there were several legitimate locations in the area for organized races—the established racetracks featured numerous different types of cars, from hopped-up street machines to elaborate dragsters and funny cars—it was also quite easy to organize illegal drag races on deserted roads on weekend nights.

A great deal of music was dedicated to this car culture. When an artist's sales dipped a bit, releasing an album with a hot rod on the cover and song titles reflecting car terminology was one way to boost those flagging sales.

Two of Brian Wilson's first collaborators were big fans of the car scene. After his falling-out with Murry Wilson, Gary Usher, Brian's first collaborator, went on to record several car tunes on his own. Los Angeles DJ Roger Christian, who was an expert on cars, was recruited by Murry Wilson, who thought the young man could work with Brian on car tunes.

"409," "Little Honda," "Shut Down," "Little Deuce Coupe," and "Little GTO" were some of the more popular car tunes of the surf era, though they were by no means the only ones that sold well. Almost all the surf bands had at least one song dedicated to automobiles on their play list and on at least one of their albums.

The movie companies picked up on this fascination with cars and pumped out a series of exploitive films, some of which had the same cast as their surf counterparts.

THE PYRAMIDS

The Pyramids, circa 1963. Front, left to right: Tom Pitman, Willy Glover, Skip Mercier, Steve Leonard. Back, on the drums: Ron McMullen.

The Pyramids were founded by Willy Glover and Skip Mercier, two young men who went to high school together in Long Beach, California. One day at school, Mercier stopped Glover in the courtyard and asked him to teach him how to play guitar. Glover showed his schoolmate what little he knew and they went their separate ways. A few months later, Mercier called Glover and asked him if he wanted to start a band. They played with a few people before settling on Ron McMullen (drums), Steve Leonard (bass), and Tom Pitman (sax).

John Hodge, a schoolmate of Glover's, became the band's manager in the following way: Even though he had no money to finance a recording session for the band, he told Glover that he was going to make him a star. Glover paid him little or no attention and continued playing his guitar for free at Lutton Beach. Soon after, Hodge managed to talk his neighbor, Paul Bochard, into putting up the money for the Pyramids to book time in a recording studio. The group recorded two Steve Leonard originals: "The Pyramid Stomp" and "Paul" (named after their benefactor). The session was a disaster; the engineer was below par, the equipment was equally substandard, and the mix was muddy, making the instruments hard to discern. Nevertheless, Hodge printed up about 250 copies on his new label, Best Records. The record got little or no airplay, and sales were negligible.

In 1963 the Pyramids were appearing regularly at dances and college frat parties. They also decided to try recording again. The original plan was to record two of Glover's tunes—"Here Comes Marsha" and "Carol Ann"—but Steve Leonard wanted to do a tune along the lines of "Pipeline." He came up with the basic idea,

The Pyramids were one of the few surf bands whose image revolved around gimmicks and onstage antics.

and with assistance from his mother and Skip Mercier, the song "Penetration" was born.

Hodge then booked them at Western Studios in Hollywood, with Chuck Britz, who had already worked with the Beach Boys, Dick Dale, and the Crossfires, as engineer. The plan was to record all three tracks, then choose the A side from the two girl songs and use "Penetration" as the B side. In the middle of the session, Glover left to get something to eat. In his absence, the group recorded "Penetration" with Mercier overdubbing the lead part. When Glover came back, the song was finished.

The cover for the Pyramids' Penetration album.

As soon as Best Records released "Penetration," radio stations outside of Los Angeles started playing the song. Eventually, Hodge took the single to KRLA and met with the rock and roll DJs Casey Kasem, Reb Foster, and Arlin Sanders. The station began playing it, promoting it enough that it debuted on the *Billboard* charts at number thirty-nine, remaining there for a few weeks before moving up. It eventually peaked at number four, and stayed in the Top Ten for thirteen weeks. The only thing that kept the song from reaching number one was the Beatles. It was at this point that John Hodge decided that they should shave their heads and wear Beatle wigs onstage, which they would remove at some point during the set. This threw a wrench into the "blond surfer" image that was prevalent at the time, but any fan of surf music knew which band was bald. He made sure the press had advance notice and even went so far as to hire girls to go wild over the boys during their "trim."

The success of "Penetration" convinced Hodge and the band that the time was right to record an album. The subsequent recording session lasted three hours. After the band left the studio, the producers took the liberty of adding to the record a few tracks the band hadn't recorded, including a Marketts outtake entitled "Outer Limits" and a Road Runners song called "Road Runnah." No one in the group knew about these added songs until the album was released, and by that time nothing could be done. There were grounds for a lawsuit, but who really wanted to sue? The artists whose tracks were added to the record received free publicity and the proper royalties, and the Pyramids had a solid album.

With the recording of the album out of the way, the Pyramids made the rounds of the television shows: *American Bandstand, The Bob Eubanks Dance Party, Shebang, The Lloyd Thaxton Show,* and *Dave Hull's Hullabaloo.* They also played shows with both Ray Charles and the Lettermen and performed for the Miss Universe contestants at a private luncheon.

Meanwhile, John Hodge was getting the lion's share of the income generated by the group. The only money the boys in the band saw was from their personal appearances. Hodge told them he was "investing" their earnings, and they kept him in his position. And Hodge's publicity stunts were not limited to the hair gags; the band also was subject to helicopter rides and elephant escorts, as well as borderline exhibitionism at the Rendezvous Ballroom (for one gig they wore trenchcoats with nothing underneath except leggings). Through Roger Christian, the group was able to meet Gary Usher, then assistant musical director at American International Pictures. He was the musical director on the upcoming film, *Bikini Beach,* and he had the band record two songs for the movie: "Bikini Drag" and "Record Run." They were also Little Stevie Wonder's backup band in the film.

Throughout the remainder of 1964, a few more records were recorded on various labels, but the band was soon to break up. Ron McMullen left in late 1964 or early 1965, and was followed in May 1965 by Glover and Leonard, who went on to form Family Cat. Mercier tried to keep the band going, but he eventually gave up. The last time they played together was in 1972.

The Crossfires

In 1981 Rhino Records reissued the Crossfires' *Out of Control.* If not for the success of the Turtles—the band later formed by two members of the Crossfires—this LP might never have made it to the record stores.

Most of the members of the Crossfires went to the same high school in Los Angeles. The band was formed by Chuck Portz (bass) and Al Nichol (guitar). The first person they asked to join was saxophonist Howard Kaylan (né Kaplan), who had been playing for only two weeks. Dale Walton (guitar) joined a few weeks later, and after Don Murray (drums), who attended a rival school across town, came on board, the band started playing hops and dances. They quickly became popular, and often had to farm out gigs to other local bands.

It was at one of the band's early shows, in the spring of 1963, that Mark Volman first saw and heard the Crossfires. A few days later in choir practice, he realized that the guy standing next to him was Howard Kaylan, a member of the band. Telling Kaylan that he thought the band was great, Volman asked if he could join. When asked what he could do, he said "Nothing!" Kaylan replied, "Terrific. Sounds promising," and invited Volman to the fraternity party the Crossfires were playing at

The Crossfires (left to right): Al Nichol, Dale Walton, Chuck Portz, Don Murray, Mark Volman, Howard Kaplan.

the University of California, Los Angeles, that weekend. Kaylan remembers Volman getting very drunk and dropping the drums down a flight of stairs, then falling down the same stairs himself. With this auspicious introduction, the band asked Volman to join; aside from destroying equipment, he was fun to be around and he was willing to load and unload the amps and other heavy equipment when the band played shows. For a much smaller cut of the door than the other band members received, he would get up and play tambourine and sing a few songs. Once his father found out what was going on, he purchased a saxophone for him, and Volman became a full partner in the band.

The band became as well known for their antics as for their music. From getting banned from some venues to having a fan club known as the Chunky Club, the band got bigger with each incident.

The band's first studio recordings were made in April 1963. With Chuck Britz at Western Studios as their engineer, the group recorded six songs in one hour. Two of the tunes from this session—"Dr. Jekyll and Mr. Hyde" b/w "Fiberglass Jungle"—were released on Capco Records. This single reached the top ten at their high school, but didn't go very far anywhere else.

The Crossfires settled into a routine in which they played the same shows for the same crowd. This continued through 1964 and into early 1965, when Reb Foster took over the managerial reins from Bert Bertrand and had the group record a few folk songs, including "It Ain't Me, Babe" by Bob Dylan. In 1965 White Whale Records released a single with the Dylan tune as the A side and a Kaylan original, "The Wandering Kind," as the B side. At the same time, the group changed their name from the Crossfires to the Turtles. This was a Reb Foster suggestion, presumably intended to get the band away from the surf association (and maybe the bad press associated with the original name).

The Crossfires, who changed their name to the Turtles and changed their musical style to be more in keeping with the new sound, were one of the few surf bands to survive the British Invasion.

In their first gig as the Turtles, they performed in green clothes and hats, but played the same songs to the same crowd. The next weekend, "It Ain't Me, Babe" hit the charts and the band hit the road.

The Turtles produced numerous hit singles, including "Happy Together." Kaylan and Volman became Flo and Eddie and have sung backing vocals on numerous projects, joining Frank Zappa's Mothers of Invention after the Turtles broke up in 1969. They did the soundtrack for the television series *Strawberry Shortcake* and sang on Bruce Springsteen's "Hungry Heart," among other projects.

Avenger VI

Although surf music had more or less peaked by 1964, there were still groups releasing albums for the next few years. Avenger VI was formed in Anaheim, California, in 1964, and at first they went the usual surf band route: playing dances, hops, and USO shows. In 1966 George Garabedian, a record producer from Mark 56 Records, which is based in Anaheim, saw the group at a Disneyland performance; he liked them and immediately took them into a studio to record an album.

Garabedian had already made arrangements with the Good Humor Ice Cream company to release the record as a promotional item from their trucks. *Real Cool Hits* was available for a short time before Good Humor folded and Mark 56 was left with a slew of albums. Today, this LP is considered a collector's item and a single copy can sell for upwards of $150.

Bob Keane and Del-Fi Records

Bob Keane's first big break in the record business came in 1952, when Artie Shaw retired and left Keane in charge of his orchestra. At the time, Keane was playing with his own band in the Los Angeles area. He ran Shaw's band for a few years before starting a label called Kean. His first major star was Sam Cooke, who had a few hits with the label before signing with RCA.

When Keane found out that his partner, who was responsible for handling the financial end of the business (paying creditors and the like), was not doing his job, Keane decided to start a new label: Del-Fi. One of the first artists signed was the up-and-coming Ritchie Valens, who was killed in a plane crash along with Buddy Holly and the Big Bopper in 1959.

Mustang Records, a Del-Fi subsidiary, produced records by the Bobby Fuller Four, whose big hit was "I Fought the Law" (later covered by the Clash). Fuller's death in 1966 was ruled a suicide, but Keane feels there's more to his death—a well-kept secret, perhaps—and he plans to make a movie on the subject. Between funerals, Keane released several surf albums, as well as hot rod tunes, Latino recordings, and the first efforts of the late, great Frank Zappa. Of the surf bands, the Lively Ones were the group with the most releases. Dave Myers and the Surftones, the Impacts, and Bruce Johnston also recorded for Del-Fi in the early 1960s.

Part of Keane's promotional efforts involved giving away hearses in cities across the United States. There were giveaways in Dallas, Pittsburgh, San Francisco, and Los Angeles, to name only a few locations.

After surf music was pushed aside by the British Invasion and Keane had burned out on the record industry, he closed up the labels for the next twenty or so years. In 1993 he started reissuing the Valens and Fuller material, as well as signing new acts. In 1994, capitalizing on the resurgence in surf music, he rereleased twelve of the surf titles. There are plans for more reissues in the future.

Bob Keane (right) with Ritchie Valens (né Valenzuela), one of many young stars whose careers Keane helped to establish.

THE END OF AN ERA

The arrival of the Beatles in 1964 not only heralded the British Invasion, but also marked the beginning of the end for surf music. While some subgenres of rock and roll managed to hang on for a little while—folk musicians, for instance, continued to draw crowds at coffeehouses, perhaps because folk had much in common with some of the music being played by the Beatles and the Rolling Stones—surf was essentially dead at this point.

Few rock and rollers who got their start in surf music had musical careers past the late sixties. Flo and Eddie remained active as session musicians and even did a stint as morning radio jocks on WXRK New York in the early 1990s.

The major record labels had always been skeptical of the national appeal of surf music. When the Beatles arrived, most groups that had been signed to the majors were either cut loose or buried on the roster. In order to adapt to the new style (and simply to survive), some of the groups made wholesale changes, generally with horrendous results. Some bands—for example, the Beach Boys and the Crossfires/Turtles—succeeded in reinventing themselves and were able to forge new careers. Artists like Dick Dale, however, were callously dropped by the major labels even though, in many cases, they were still selling albums. And independent labels, the mainstay for many surf bands and other alternative acts that the majors were unwilling to support, were slowly but surely falling victim to poor business management and the fickle teenage market. The roster for many of these labels consisted of only one band, and when that band broke up there was no reason to maintain the label (and no means of generating revenue). Because many of the records released by these labels had been used for promotional purposes, there was often no money being made by these organizations. For these reasons, when surf music finally died out, many of these labels went out of business.

During the heyday of surf music, very few of the performers were over twenty years old; for these young folks the future meant college or the Vietnam war, and few could see beyond to what life would be like in the next decade. Few of these musicians went on to careers in music that put them in the public eye.

The 1990s have seen a resurgence in surf music. Labels like Bob Keane's Del-Fi Records have reissued their surf titles, and new groups, heirs to the surf legacy, have been signed to new independent labels. Bands like the Phantom Surfers and Laika & the Cosmonauts (who are from Finland!) are now recording and touring regularly. Some of the original surf bands, such as the Chantays, have reunited for live gigs, while others, like the Bel-airs, have rereleased some of their old titles on independent labels (the Bel-air record is accompanied by a seventy-two-page book written by Bel-airs cofounder Paul Johnson). And with the advent of cable television (not to mention the frequent use of surf music in television commercials, such as Oxy acne medicine's use of "Wipeout" and Sunkist soda's use of "Good Vibrations"), the genre is no longer limited to the southern portions of the California coast.

The masked Phantom Surfers, who come from San Francisco, are one of today's hottest surf bands.

And while no one can say for sure how long this trend will last, one thing is certain: as long as there are garages, guitars, and rock and roll, there will be kids trying to figure out the guitar riff to "Pipeline" and doing their best to pick out the familiar notes to "Wipe-Out."

The lack of vocals in surf music appeals to bands from around the globe, who know that a rock and roll band must have hits in English-speaking countries in order to succeed. Laika & the Cosmonauts, who hail from Finland, are one of the bigger non-American surf groups of the nineties.

Bibliography

Blair, John. *The Illustrated Discography of Surf Music, 1961–1965.* Los Angeles: John W. Blair, Jr., 1983.

_____, and Stephen J. McParland. *The Illustrated Discography of Hot Rod Music, 1961–1965.* Ann Arbor, Mich.: Popular Culture, Ink, 1990.

Dalley, Robert J. *Surfin' Guitars: Instrumental Bands of the Sixties.* Los Angeles: Surf Publications, 1988.

Gaines, Steven. *Heroes & Villains: The True Story of the Beach Boys.* New York: New American Library, 1986.

Kolanjian, Steve. *Surf City: The Best of Jan & Dean* (liner notes). Hollywood, Calif.: Capitol/EMI, 1990.

Leaf, David. *The Beach Boys Good Vibrations: Thirty Years of the Beach Boys* (liner notes). Hollywood, Calif.: Capitol Records, 1993.

Pareles, Jon. "Surfin' Again." *The New York Times,* sec. 9. Sunday, May 1, 1994.

Wilson, Brian, with Todd Gold. *Wouldn't It Be Nice: My Own Story.* New York: HarperCollins, 1991.

Suggested Reading

Blaine, Hal. *Hal Blaine and the Wrecking Crew.* Emeryville, Calif.: Mix Books, 1990.

Crenshaw, Marshall. *Hollywood Rock: A Guide to Rock and Roll in the Movies.* New York: HarperCollins, 1994.

Leaf, David. *The Beach Boys and the California Myth.* New York: Grosset & Dunlap, 1978.

Ward, Ed, Geoffrey Stokes, and Ken Tucker. *Rock of Ages.* New York: Rolling Stone Press, 1986.

White, Timothy. *Rock Lives.* New York: Henry Holt, 1990.

Suggested Listening

The Beach Boys. *Good Vibrations: Thirty Years of the Beach Boys.* Capitol.

The Bel-airs. *The Origins of Surf Music 1960–1963.* Iloki.

Dick Dale. *Anthology.* Rhino.

_____. *Tribal Thunder.* Hightone.

Dave Myers and the Surftones. *Hangin' Twenty.* Del-Fi.

The Phantom Surfers. *18 Deadly Ones.* Norton.

Ronnie & the Daytonas. *G.T.O.* Mala.

The Trashmen. *Surfin' Bird.* Sundazed.

Various artists. *Big Surf*. Ace.

Various artists. *Rock Instrumental Classics, Vol. 5: Surf*. Rhino.

Various artists. *Surf & Drag, Vol. 1*. Sundazed.

Various artists. *Surf Legends (And Rumors)*. Del Rack/DCC.

Suggested Surf Films

Listed after the date for each film's release are the featured musical performers.

Beach Ball. Paramount, 1965.
The Supremes, the Righteous Brothers, the Four Seasons, the Hondells, the Walker Brothers

Beach Blanket Bingo. American International Pictures, 1965.
The Hondells, Donna Loren

The Beach Boys: An American Band. High Ridge Productions, 1985.
Follows the career of the band from inception through the mid-1980s

Beach Party. American International Pictures, 1964.
Dick Dale & His Del-tones, Brian Wilson in a cameo role

Bikini Beach. American International Pictures, 1964.
The Pyramids, the Exciter Band, Little Stevie Wonder

Dead Man's Curve. Made-for-television movie, 1978.
Jan & Dean, as portrayed by Richard Hatch and Bruce Davidson, respectively

Endless Summer. Bruce Brown production, 1964.
No bands performed in the movie, but it was one of the earliest surf films and has held up well as a benchmark for other surf films.

Gidget. Columbia Pictures, 1959.
The Four Preps

Girls on the Beach. Paramount, 1965.
The Beach Boys, the Crickets, Leslie Gore

How to Stuff a Wild Bikini. American International Pictures, 1965.
The Kingsmen

Muscle Beach Party. American International Pictures, 1964.
Dick Dale & His Del-tones, Little Stevie Wonder, Donna Loren. Frankie Avalon and Annette Funicello, who were in all the abovementioned A.I.P. films, both released soundtrack albums from this movie

The T.A.M.I. Show. Electonovision, 1964.
The Beach Boys and Jan & Dean represented the surf contingent. Other acts included Chuck Berry, James Brown, and the Rolling Stones.

Photography Credits

© Greg Allen/Retna: p. 12

© Archive Photos/American Stock: p. 6

Courtesy of Hal Blaine: pp. 16, 17, 36, 37, 38

© Jay Blakesberg/Retna: p. 39 bottom

Robert J. Dalley Collection: pp. 9 bottom, 14, 50 bottom, 51, 52, 53, 54, 56, 57 top, 58, 60, 61 top

Courtesy of Del-Fi Records: p. 65

Frank Driggs Collection: p. 66

FPG International: pp. 22, 41

© Dennis Hallinan/FPG International: p. 10

Courtesy of Hightone Records: p. 19

© Dan Lyons: p. 59

© Michael Ochs Archive: pp. 2, 8, 9 top, 11, 13, 18, 23 bottom, 25, 26, 31, 33, 34 bottom, 43, 45 all, 46, 47, 48, 63

© Bob Patterson/Globe Photos: p. 39 top

Neal Peters Collection: p. 28

Photofest: pp. 7, 21, 32, 34 top, 35

© Pictorial Press/Star File: p. 20

© Michael Putland/Retna: p. 40

Rob Santos Collection: pp. 15, 50 top, 55, 57 bottom, 61 bottom, 64 bottom, 67 top

© Sterling/McFadden/Globe Photos: p. 23 top

© Thor Svenson/Globe Photos: p. 42

© Gene Trindl/Globe Photos: p. 64 top

© UPI/Bettman: p. 49

Courtesy of Upstart Records: p. 67 bottom

Index